Attack on Privacy

Attack on Privacy

John Curtis Raines

JUDSON PRESS, VALLEY FORGE

ATTACK ON PRIVACY

Library of Congress Cataloging in Publication Data

Raines, John C.
    Attack on privacy.

    Includes bibliographical references.
    1. Privacy, Right of—United States. 2. United
States—Social conditions—1960-   I. Title.
JC599.U5R24   323.44'0973   73-16691
ISBN 0-8170-0621-4

Printed in the U.S.A.

Acknowledgments

I wish to express my gratitude to Temple University which granted me a study leave for the fall of 1973, making it possible to complete this manuscript with dispatch. I want also to thank the United Presbyterian Church in the U.S.A., who through their Special Task Force on Privacy of the Advisory Council on Church and Society first persuaded me to focus my attention on this issue. Members of that Task Force will find many of their insights in these pages.

I acknowledge with gratitude permission to use in this book substantial portions of my article "Community and Privacy" (reprinted from the December 25, 1972, issue of *Christianity and Crisis,* copyright © 1972 by Christianity and Crisis, Inc.) and my article "Middle America: Up Against the Wall and Going Nowhere" (Copyright 1973 Christian Century Foundation; reprinted from the May 2, 1973, issue of *The Christian Century*).

Finally, my gratitude would remain remiss without also thanking the students of Temple University for the instruction received from them on the arts of surviving bureaucracy and expertise, and, not least, to the patience and forbearance of my wife and children.

To my parents, who gave me my first education, and the generation of the sixties who gave me my second.

Table of Contents

Preface

Attack on Privacy
Space to Be Human—A Basic Right

We are not wanted as citizens anymore. We are wanted as passive system inhabitants. In return we are promised a plentitude of pleasantries, weekend diversions, and an ever expanding variety of legal opiates. The only thing we must give up is the already unfashionable notion of our own seriousness and integrity. We grow modern and behavioral. We receive our place in reality as subjects of bureaucratic manipulation. De-privatized, we come to feel "at home"—integrated, immediate, and uncomplicatedly healthy minded.

While we turn public, discovering that our only "friend" with any power to help us is the social system itself, the world of public decisions which shapes that system turns private. Organized interest groups take over the funding of what we once thought of as public elections. Federal agencies administrate for the benefit of their administered clientele. Managerial elites commute between executive boardrooms in industry and law, and top administrative positions in government—a symbiosis of the hierarchies. The result? Citizenship is replaced by the trickle-down rewards of established interests and advantages. Everything runs smoothly. We become not just modern, but also sophisticated, hard-nosed, and practical. The world appears tamed, homogenized: like Eden before rebellion, blessedly predictable.

And that is where we are, or where we are heading: the reversal of public and private worlds, persons turned public, politics becom-

11

ing private. We are adjusting to the new administrative state. You ask for signs of the times?

—Watergate is one, with its undermining of the public political process for the benefit of established private advantages.

—The ubiquitous credit card is another, tracking the patterns of our personal and associational activities, rendering us machine readable and retained.

—The computer is a third, with its possibilities for networking diverse personal data systems: bank records and credit ratings, educational and psychological testings, employment histories, political views, and protest activities.

So private men become public records while public power is secreted into closed systems of private benefit. Vital selfhood and vital citizenship bear a common life and suffer in our day a common loss.

This relationship between selfhood and citizenship places the issue of privacy in a new light. In the past the issue has been dealt with mostly by legal specialists or by scholars studying total institutions like asylums and prisons. This type of inquiry has led to practical benefits in legal and institutional practice. But it has prevented the issue of privacy from being used to reflect more comprehensively upon our cultural system as a whole. The overall drift of our society interests me here. A review of the recent career of privacy provides a revealing commentary upon that drift. For individual and associational privacy are the cradle of both personal vitality and that social distance necessary for effective citizen advice and consent. Privacy, then, becomes a key political issue because it bears upon the fundamental logic of not just our own but of all high-technology societies.

Still, what really gives pause is the degree to which the public acquiesces to and even welcomes this administrative invasion, this managerial takeover of our effectiveness as persons. We are grateful that others carry the burden of our lives! To understand this acquiescence, we must examine the loss of confidence in meaningful selfhood that haunts the development of the human psyche in our times, a spiritual development which seeks its consolation in a sophisticated hedonism or in fetishisms of ideology or the occult. Both represent an embracing of self-loss that points to a deeper surrender of the spirit, to a panic before our exposure, a giving up on the lonely burden of transcendence. Privacy is a matter of politics, but in the end it is a matter of the spirit.

To sum up, because of new technologies in the collection of personal data and because of a law-and-order mentality that views opposition as subversive, we are undergoing a sharply increased invasion of individual and group privacy (chapter 1). This loss of privacy both reflects and furthers the logic of a more pervasive social process which is moving our culture in the direction of an administrative state and toward the privatization of public power (chapter 2). This transformation of the public world into a realm of private management requires that personal reserve, together with the intervening communal structures that maintain social distance, be undermined. This renders the social world flat, emptied of any resisting pockets of personal or communal loyalty, but at the price of basic self-esteem and those civil liberties essential to a relatively open and democratic society (chapters 3 and 4). This reversal of public and private worlds reflects a loss of confidence at the spiritual level concerning our seriousness and integrity as selves. Humiliated as to our significance in the abyss of time and space we become embarrassed, humble, deprived of the courage to affirm ourselves (chapter 5). Should we decide, however, for the protection of privacy and the reassertion of ourselves as selves and citizens, there are several practical actions in law and politics that need our corrective effort. But in the end, the rehabilitation of a private self in a public world remains dependent upon a revival of man's sense of his own inner depths, his transcendence and inalienable dignity (chapter 6).

1

Dossier
Prisons

"The whole dossier continues to circulate, as the regular official routine demands, passing on to the higher Courts, being referred to the lower ones again, and thus swinging backwards and forwards with greater or smaller oscillations, longer or shorter delays. . . . A detached observer might sometimes fancy that the whole case had been forgotten, the documents lost, and the acquittal made absolute. No one really acquainted with the Court could think such a thing. No document is ever lost, the Court never forgets anything. One day— quite unexpectedly—some Judge will take up the documents. . . ." "And the case begins all over again?" asked K. almost incredulously. "Certainly," said the painter.[1]

—Franz Kafka

Who watches whom? Who has a right to know what about us? These questions are increasingly determinative of the freedom and self-determination we are permitted in our everyday lives. A New York Port Authority police lieutenant recently found this out. He was observed participating, out of uniform, in a one-day picketing by rank-and-file policemen against the Port Authority. The protest resulted in higher wages for the police, none of whom were disciplined for their actions. However, despite an excellent overall employment rating, the police lieutenant received an evaluation report from one of his superiors stating that he was an "irresponsi- ble commander." When he retired a few years later, he was unable to get a job in several private security agencies because his evaluation file had been widely circulated outside the Port Authority. He was caught in a "dossier prison," a prison constructed from the subjective opinion of a superior concerning a

15

constitutionally protected activity, a prison nonetheless from which there was small chance of successful escape!

Who watches whom—

the kind of information sought and filed—

its accuracy and dissemination—

not so much the exotic affairs of the criminal, the subversive or suspected radical, as the everyday stuff out of which our jobs, our financial credit, and our educational opportunities are increasingly constructed—

not just the profile, but evermore the *raw material* of our personal destinies is at stake.

Why Is Privacy an Issue?

We are inevitably private persons by the simple fact that we inhabit separate bodies. However close we may otherwise become, we live by separate schedules. Martin Luther put it plainly: "Each man dies alone; there I cannot go with you nor you with me." But we are private persons who need also to disclose ourselves, share our secrets, seek the comfort of human companionship, and in other ways depart our solitude. Privacy becomes an issue because of this dual nature of our lives. We want to know and be known by those whom we choose to share our intimacy. But in order that we may *choose,* we must defend ourselves against nonchalant or forced disclosure. The zone of personal privacy preserves this possibility of intimate community. Its trespass, if sustained, exposes and withers the experience of intimacy and leaves us more public and surface persons.

But the right to privacy refers to more than personal relations. It is a cultural and political matter as well. It is a cultural matter because the bureaucratic form of social organization, which today characterizes all advanced industrial nations, is in many respects of a spirit alien to privacy. Bureaucracy needs to unveil the inner spaces of its clientele in order to forecast its future behavior and so manage accurately the diversity of human activity. As the sociologist Charles Horton Cooley has seen: "Underlying all formalism, indeed, is the fact that it is psychically cheap; it substitutes the outer for the inner as more tangible, more capable of being held before the mind without fresh expense of thought and feeling. . . ."² Privacy is at odds with efficiency of administration, with the logic of executive control. As such, it becomes a *political* issue as well.

The preservation of human autonomy is as dependent upon privacy of associational life as upon personal privacy. Vital persons depend upon vital associations, as surely as the opposite of individuality is not community but the lonely crowd. Lively associational life keeps political loyalties and identities complex, less than total, and thus free. For this reason democratic rule has seemed to many to depend fundamentally upon this multiplicity of "living spaces," which maintain distance and reserve over against an unreserved attachment to the state. Unfortunately, a law-and-order mentality tends to view such hesitancy as something less than full patriotism and perhaps even subversive.

Privacy, then, arises as a personal, a cultural, and a political issue. Still, it is likely to arise as an issue *for us* only when it begins to touch upon our private civilian lives.

The computerized society

We already live in a computerized society today. It is the rare American who does not dwell in the shadow of his dossier, and more likely several of them. Why? A partial answer can be found in the reply received by a Long Island couple from a local authority. The entire ninth-grade class, of which their daughter was a member, was subjected without parental consent to the highly personal and probing Minnesota Multiphasic Personality Test. When these parents asked why the test had to be given, the reply was, "In these matters it is best to trust the judgment of the educators."

In urban, mobile, highly complex societies the collection of data and its rapid and accurate transfer become key instruments in the efficient administration of society. And it is this "administration of society" with which we increasingly interact, the place where our basic human needs—educational, financial, medical, etc.—meet the given structures of community care and provision. More and more interdependent, while at the same moment more and more unknown to each other face to face, we confront the fundamental conundrum of modern society which sets such high priority on data collection and its efficient interchange. More of us comes to reside, so to speak, in our Social Security and credit card numbers because more of us becomes fundamentally exposed there. The number is the place where we plug into the social system we depend upon for the service of our everyday needs.

At first glance this growth of social administration seems but an extension and refinement of the evolutionary direction of our species as a whole. Genetically and instinctually deprived at birth of the behavioral encoding we need to know in order to survive, culture becomes our 'survival substitute, a system by which to compile, transmit, and refine information. Put simply, we are creatures who have to learn *how* to share our world in order to live. (See chapter 3 for a more detailed explanation of this point.)

Still, the history of human cultural experiments documents a need for personal privacy as well as public participation, for individual solitude and reserve. Privacy can't be passed off as a mere fetish of bourgeois individualism, the subjective introversion of objective property relations. Historical anthropology clearly shows that even in highly communal and tribal societies, with no developed division of labor or money economy, there are still highly elaborate rituals for maintaining personal distance and reserve.[3]

We belong to a social system of informational interchange, yes; but we belong to it also, or seek to do so, *as persons.* And it is this latter need and right that seems trespassed by the too routine response of the Long Island school official. There is a taken-for-granted use of new methods in psychological testing and categorization without careful balancing of the rights of personal reserve against the needs (if there are any legitimate ones in this case) of social administration. Precisely here the question of privacy is posed with increasing sharpness: at the juncture of new technologies of information handling and what one author referred to as the human need for "preserves of individual reserve."

New technologies and old restraints

The feeling is growing among those best informed that we are at a critical parting of the way, and that the logic of the new data systems if extended another few years without careful control will yield an unsought but inescapable Dossiered Society. We have arrived at this situation because of the interchange between a revolution in technologies of data handling—which outstrip

inherited mechanisms for the preservation of individual reserve—
and a widespread, increased willingness to ignore traditional
standards of restraint against the invasion of privacy. This
combination has carried us, rather suddenly, to the prospect of
what one expert has called "the fishbowl environment."

Nowhere is the human effect of the new information technology
better illustrated than in the phenomenal growth of the credit
industry. Take the Credit Data Corporation, which has over thirty
million files and adds seven million each year. Such high volume
and centralization of information bits (a credit file will include
information about job, salary, length of time on present job,
marital status, a list of present and past debts and their payment
history, any criminal record, lawsuits of any kind, and any real
estate) is unthinkable except in the age of the computer dossier.

An extension of this same effect is the automated credit card and
reservations systems that, largely unnoticed, render our everyday
lives increasingly "visible" and machine-retained. Where we
traveled, on what day, who sat beside us, what hotel we stayed in,
who stayed there at the same time, where we ate and with whom,
what football game we attended or what play or concert, and who
else was there—all of this now becomes a matter of public record.
Put this together with the ready access by officials to our bank
checking accounts retained on microfilm, and the log of our long-
distance phone calls preserved in computer readouts, and you have
attained a strikingly detailed profile of our personal and
associational life: the habits, acquaintances, life-style, charitable
and political preferences of millions of Americans. Perhaps we
have a "right to be let alone," but the means of truly being alone, of
leaving "no tracks," become increasingly scarce. Moreover, there
are those who are convinced that many of us do not deserve and
should not enjoy any such right in the first place.

Because of a law-and-order mentality which tends to view vocal
dissent as politically subversive, there has been a steady erosion by
government administrators of such traditional preserves of privacy
as political opinion and expressions of public concern. We can
find an example of this in the widespread photographing and
selective dossiering of participants at Earth Day rallies. Such
things as planning a Boy Scout trip to the Soviet Union can earn
you a complete government investigation and indexing. If you are
a college professor, the local switchboard operator may be

monitoring your calls. Or you may have a full-fledged FBI file opened on your daughter if you are a U.S. Congressman who happens to disagree with the administration's war policy.[4]

Even more to the point is the testimony of Christopher Pyle, a former army intelligence officer, before a Senate committee. He said:

> The Army maintains files on the membership, ideology, program, and practices of virtually every activist political group in the country. These include not only such violence-prone organizations as the Minutemen and the Revolutionary Action Movement (RAM), but such nonviolent groups as the Southern Christian Leadership Conference, Clergy and Laymen United Against the War in Vietnam, the American Civil Liberties Union, Women Strike for Peace, and the National Association for the Advancement of Colored People.[5]

Shortly after these revelations were made, then Secretary of Defense Melvin Laird ordered all such surveillance stopped. But a corner had been turned. Even though one can give all this a charitable estimate as the overzealous response of some otherwise well-meaning public officials to the urban riots, youth revolt, and war protests that so traumatized our nation in the sixties; yet, the gravest danger sometimes comes not from malicious intent but from well-meaning government response which overshoots itself.

Unfortunately, there is also mounting evidence (which takes a curiously determined nonchalance to ignore) that on the part of some, this massive spasm of surveillance is not so much innocent industriousness as a calculated policy of political pacification, the conscious cultivation of a "chilling effect." Consider a directive, sent by the agent in charge at the Philadelphia office of the FBI to operatives in the field, urging a step-up of interviews with political dissidents. Such a policy is "in order," the memo urges,

> for plenty of reasons, chief of which are [sic!] it will enhance the paranoia endemic in these circles and will further serve to get the point across there is an FBI Agent behind every mailbox. In addition, some will be overcome by the overwhelming personalities of the contacting agent and volunteer to tell all— perhaps on a continuing basis.[6]

It does little good, I suppose, to point out that such a policy contradicts the Constitution of the United States. After all, it's not the protection of constitutionally guaranteed behavior that is of interest to the initiating party, but the psychological inhibition of its expression.

This chilling effect is well known. It is not so different from that everyday feeling of helplessness we have as we fill out endless varieties of official forms and otherwise flounder through the widening web of information systems that locate or mislocate us beyond our will and wish. We become inmates of a *dossier prison.*

Whether the effect be upon our private or our political lives, this exposure before and engulfment within multiple informational systems should occasion sober reflection as we contemplate the implications of the psychologist Sidney Jourard's remarks about life in a prison:

> The whole process of a person's becoming a unit in an institution is one of divesting himself of his private existence. . . . He has a being-for-the-institution; he is a "warm body," a source of behavior that may be of use and that must be no trouble to the institution. Beyond this, his being has no value.[7]

So saying, it is appropriate for those of us who think well of our freedom, prizing ourselves as personal centers of independent value, to consider the grounds and warrants of our claim and our right as free citizens to demand official protection of our privacy.

Why Is Privacy Important?

> The one thing in the world, of value,
> is the active soul.
> —Ralph Waldo Emerson

Privacy is the cradle both of vital personality and of the social distance necessary to maintain effective citizenship. In this way privacy becomes the common foundation of two of our prized cultural values: individual *dignity* and public *freedom*. Let us take each in turn.

The active soul

This idea is likely to strike a sophisticated modern as somewhat quaint, a kind of nostalgic sigh from out of a simpler past. We live, after all, in a newer and braver world, an age of motivational research, of TV advertising and politics by calculated image, an age, in short, of man's general loss of confidence in any "inner space" that has much public weight or clout. And this is one of those fundamental "facts" of the social landscape—as much so as computers—which undermines the processes of privacy in our day. It is not only that we have less privacy today, but we also increasingly appear to ourselves as *being* less private, and so without grounds for complaint.

By way of contrast, privacy has seemed in the past inextricably related to personal dignity and autonomy. Professor Edward Bloustein speaks for this older tradition when he says:

> The man who is compelled to live every minute of his life among others and whose every need, thought, desire, fancy or gratification is subject to public scrutiny, has been deprived of his individuality and human dignity. Such an individual merges with the mass. His opinions, being public, tend never to be different; his aspirations, being known, tend always to be conventionally accepted ones; his feelings, being openly exhibited, tend to lose their quality of unique personal warmth and to become the feelings of every man. Such a being, although sentient, is fungible; he is not an individual.[8]

Privacy is linked here to the idea of man as self-acting and self-directing. The personhood of the individual as something at least in part independent and bearing a separate value from the encompassing social system is its object and claim. Thomas Emerson of Yale Law School puts it this way: "The right of privacy . . . establishes an area excluded from the collective life, not governed by the rules of collective living. It is based upon premises of individualism, that the society exists to promote the worth and the dignity of the individual."[9] This domain of the un-programmed, of the potentially unmanipulable and unpredictable, provides the "hole in the web of reality" through which the individual emerges with power and significance apart from his generalized social background.

The self is not simply a reflected being but also a being-in-itself that reflects back upon and changes its cultural setting. The Latin American educator Paulo Freire, in a quite sobering parallel between his part of the world and our own, uses this same distinction to identify the fundamental movement of human liberation under the conditions of colonial oppression. And that is the struggle of men to become "considerers of the world," "subjects of history" rather than its passive object, not just an empty space through which something else passes, but their own space and project of living. Psychologist Sidney Jourard speaks to this. He argues: "Privacy is essential for that disclosure which illumines a man's being-for-himself, changes his being-for-others, and potentiates desirable growth of his personality."[10]

Personal reserve, having and holding "our own place," is intimately connected with this sense of personal power and effectiveness. Exhibitionism and voyeurism are contrasting illustrations of a basic ineffectiveness of personal life, and panic before its exercise in others. The one wants to get hold of everybody else's secrets, while the other wants to get rid of his own. For without privacy there is response but no orchestration, no demand for self-dramatization, no call for a boldness of the self with itself. Where everything is seen, everything is seen through; the burdens all are lifted.

Privacy displays itself, then, as one of the fundamental categories of man's being as man, a witness to his establishment in reality without which he begins to lose a sense of himself and resent the place in reality held aside by others. This is what the sociologist Edward Shils is trying to get at in arguing:

> The "social space" around an individual, the recollection of his past, his conversation, his body and its image, all *belong* to him. . . . He possesses them and is entitled to possess them by virtue of the charisma which is inherent in his existence as an individual soul. . . .[11]

This "charisma of an individual soul" points to a kind of fundamental piety which is *awe before the presence of another's presence and reserve concerning one's own presence.* It is the opposite of that kind of jealousy of spirit which finds no mystery in itself, or is terrified by it, and out of that internal deprivation cannot bear the idea that another might have "hidden spaces" in which he finds enrichment and strength.

Awe before the being of another and reserve concerning one's own being—here is a sign, a warning written over man's interaction with his fellows, of the right of self-defense against the imperialism of relentless inquiry, against all watching that would everywhere follow, probe, and hold a person within its sovereign gaze. Curiously, the Old Testament remembers God, too, as refusing this kind of power. "And the Lord God made for Adam and for his wife garments of skins, and clothed them" (Genesis 3:21). Thus, Genesis speaks of God's first gift to man besides the gift of existence itself as the right of reticence—before the eyes of each other, even before the eyes of God.

Privacy bears upon this power of man's spirit. It is the claim to a transcendent right—the conviction of an inviolable self-esteem, the courage to belong to oneself. It was no accident, therefore, that in order to humiliate and break their spirits, the Nazi death camps first stripped new arrivals and then caused them to pass naked before the eyes of their "judges" as part of their initiation into hell.

Privacy is a constitutive part of the being of man as man, and its radical trespass inevitably sounds an echo, however distant, of the executioner—the one who despises man's manness and wishes only to humiliate and crush it.

This threat has caused Senator Sam Ervin, chairman of the Senate Subcommittee on Constitutional Rights, to complain that

> any practice, any act, any threat which reduces a man in dignity, which limits the freedom of his conscience or his capacity for thinking and acting for himself— this is wrong—whether it be termed an invasion of his privacy or tyranny over his mind.[12]

This brings us to the *political meaning of privacy*, a meaning that is most clearly reflected in the issue of associational privacy and the role of voluntary associations in our American experiment in democracy.

Privacy and freedom

The idea is quite simple, confirmed by common sense and practical experience. First, the vitality of voluntary associations determines in large part the texture of the common life. And second, this vitality of associational life is dependent upon privacy of community.

As members of voluntary communities we establish ourselves at a certain distance from the general social system. We give ourselves room thereby not simply to subsist as passive system-inhabitants, isolated units of social administration, but to stand over against these public determinations in subsidiary communities of self-definition and loyalty. The plain truth is we do not become and remain strong individuals, and strong in our individuality, alone or individually, but only as participants in vital communities of shared values. Privacy presupposes community. Its enemy is the lonely crowd.

With our country not yet half a century old, Alexis de Tocqueville saw in such voluntary associations the human fuel of our attempt at democracy. "Nothing, in my opinion," he said, "is more deserving of our attention than the intellectual and moral associations of America."[13] Without them, he was persuaded, there would be a closing-in and totalizing of the context of everyday life, a loss of that intermediary network of human mutualities and interdependencies   that   pluralize   the   social   landscape.

Associational vitality is essential to democracy. Without it we become mass man, not common participants but passive and isolated observers.

Privacy, in turn, is essential to this vitality of associational life. Supreme Court Justice Harlan argued this point saying *(NAACP v. Alabama):*

> This Court has recognized the vital relationship between freedom to associate and privacy in one's associations. . . . Inviolability of privacy in group association may in many circumstances be indispensable to freedom of association, particularly where a group espouses dissident beliefs.[14]

Privacy of association is important because it provides space for sheltered experiment. It provides a place for testing ideas with some assurance of a secluded comradeship of correction which frees us from the fear of ridicule and so makes psychic room for trying new opinions, or altering old ones, before hardening them into a public stance. As Alan Westin of Columbia Law School concludes,

> Freedom of communion means, clearly and unquestionably, freedom to speak, debate, and write in privacy, to share confidences with intimates and confidants, and to prepare positions in groups and institutions for presentation to the public at a later point.[15]

This right to decide when we are "going public," to keep private the conversations with trusted colleagues, is what extends and enlarges us as persons. Monologue, on the other hand, always suffers from a certain moral poverty. It does not know how to escape the logic of its own unfolding. It can gain no distance upon itself. Governments which take an oppressive attitude toward vital associational life therefore encourage a kind of moral infantilism in their citizens. Justice Lewis Powell grasped this insight in arguing a 1972 wiretap case. "The price of lawful public dissent," he said, "must not be a dread of subjection to an unchecked surveillance power. Nor must the fear of unauthorized official eavesdropping deter vigorous citizen dissent and discussion of Government action in private conversation."[16] Democracy requires personal privacy and privacy of community.

Now this system of private associations is almost the reverse of a certain administrative or executive mentality which looks upon the clutter of multiple associations as a mess to be worried and managed into a unified system of efficiency. Karl Mannheim refers to this passion of the managerial mind "to turn all problems of politics into problems of administration." It is a mind set which tends, as he says, "to generalize its own experience and to overlook the fact that the realm of administration and of smoothly functioning order represents only a part of the total political reality."[17] Privacy of association requires that a certain price be paid in efficiency of social management. Still, as Supreme Court Justice Jackson noted, "Simplicity of administration is a merit that does not inhere in a federal system of government."[18]

Behind such a judgment lies a deeper-rooted claim about the nature of man who, even in the midst of his social determinants, is viewed also as a kind of freedom event. Implicit in American constitutional law is this notion of a destiny for man higher than the pleasantries of an efficiency system that can deliver the goods by day and softly lull us to sleep at night. It is what Ralph Waldo Emerson spoke of as man's "active soul." The framers of our Constitution saw man as naturally active, a builder, as it were, of the New Jerusalem. Implied throughout their argument for personal and communal independence is this basic wager: that man holds his citizenship not simply in the nation as realized in today's headline and political administration but finally in a commonwealth of wider and more permanent significance. Put simply, the meaning of America was for it to become the homeland of human aspiration, a truly *New World*.

Admittedly we have a long ways to go. Thus, the style of our traveling is all the more important. Freedom is not only the basis of privacy, but also privacy preserves this freedom in social reality. We must attend now to some of its more striking contemporary invasions.

Types of Privacy Invasion

We are indeed moving into a new world, but hardly the sort envisioned by the framers of our Constitution. We have a new world of computer technology and the growth of government willingness to treat us not as fellow citizens but as passive system clientele, as objects of public administration. *We are on our way toward becoming a transparent society of profit and public pacification.* Evidence for this can be viewed under three sub-headings: (1) transparent society, (2) record prisons, and (3) suspect citizenship.

Transparent society

Author and social critic Michael Harrington names this issue quite precisely. He points out:

> Bureaucracy is the only way to coordinate the complex functions of a modern economy and society and therefore cannot be dismissed with a curse. Yet it is also an enormous potential source of arbitrary, impersonal power which folds, bends, spindles and mutilates individuals but keeps IBM cards immaculate.[19]

Besides govenment, commerce and industry compose probably the most massive bureaucracy with which our lives routinely interact. To meet its own internal needs, the commercial world practices a kind of targeting upon us as its system inhabitants and clients. This targeting takes place where we enter into commerce, and these days that's mostly by way of our credit and our credentialing. In this fashion we become system relevant, locatable as public and commercial creatures. Ralph Nader sees the implications of this "record-texture" of our public lives. He points out that "anyone possessing an individual's bank records—now extensively recorded on computers—can reconstruct his associations, movements, habits, and life-style."[20] Add to these millions of bank-account profiles the over one hundred million files maintained by the member agencies of the Associated Credit Bureaus of America or the millions of life-insurance investigations either in or going into computerized dossiers, and you begin to get a quite detailed picture of almost all of us routinely moving through the commercial information systems. The walls of our personal lives have become increasingly transparent.

Take, for example, the kind of data which life-insurance investigators gather as a matter of their daily business. Information not only on one's health but also about his drinking habits (how often, how much, alone or with others, etc.), salary, debts, net worth, domestic troubles, reputation, associates, manner of living, and standing in the community will be solicited from neighbors and associates and fed into the information network. This "soft data" may come to rest side by side with the so-called "hard data" of a psychological test given years before by a school or later by an employment agency or as part of the evaluation procedures of one's employer. This information might pass before the eyes of someone who is an expert neither in information science nor in psychological testing and yet must make a decision vital to our interests. Increasingly our reputations are constructed out of these multiple credentialings—old and new—most of which were not intended to rest side by side, or for a use other than the original. Arthur Miller of Harvard Law School comments laconically upon the accuracy of such personal profiling:

> As strange as it may sound, many personnel managers [and others, we might add] are purporting to pass on the level of an individual's "neuroticism," "alienation," "drive," and "stability" by a process that often is not appreciably more scientific than measuring the size and shape of the subject's head.[21]

Yet, it is by means of such "testing" that our official—i.e., system-relevant—personalities are more and more established.

The result of all this is that we are rendered more public, machine profiled and retained, and by the interfacing of data banks and the standardization of information languages, "available" beyond our knowledge and will. We are also haunted by the specter of an image of ourselves that is taken totally out of context or bears, perhaps, but the remotest semblance of relevance or accuracy. In a society advancing toward a transparent world, in which *to be is to be seen*, we can't even be sure that the glass won't turn out to be more like fun-house mirrors than like spectacles.

But dossiering gets us into an issue beyond that of the accuracy of information and its appropriate interpretation. It raises the issue of the type of personal data that is collected in the first place. Senator Ervin has brought into public light the highly questionable types of personal self-disclosure requested and/or required for employment at various federal agencies. A list of some of the statements prospective employees were asked to respond to is revealing in more than one way.

My sex life is satisfactory.
I have never been in trouble because of my sex behavior.
Everything is turning out just like the prophets of the Bible said it would.
I loved my father.
I am very strongly attracted to members of my own sex.
I go to church almost every week.
I believe in the second coming of Christ.
I believe in a life hereafter.
I have never indulged in any unusual sex practices.
I am worried about sex matters.
I am very religious (more than most people).
I loved my mother.
I believe there is a Devil and a Hell in afterlife.[22]

Hundreds of federal officials interacting with thousands of prospective employees in this kind of peep-show/catechism combination would be an enormously humorous scene except for the fact that it's actually happening.

This test is a dramatic example of the invasion of privacy that remains far too often simply a matter of routine in psychological and personality testing. "What do people, and especially 'official' people, have a right to ask me?" This question, much more than it does, should mark the effective borders of a sense of individual dignity and reserve, a line carefully defined and not to be breached. "You have no business asking that!" is a sign these days not of outdated modesty but of a sophisticated sense of self-esteem.

That we have a long ways to go in this matter is graphically illustrated by our seemingly passive acceptance of *psychological hard-sell advertising* which shows no modesty at all in turning the private space of our inner vulnerabilities into the public workhouses of consumer appetite. It is not, evidently, just the outside of us that's on display in the new transparent society, but our insides as well!

Take a recent TV commerical for a patent medicine. It shows a retired but still vigorous couple touring the countryside in their camper. The husband, balding, but otherwise pictured as obviously robust, comes over and puts his hands lovingly on the shoulders of his wife, who is strikingly well-preserved for her supposedly fifty or so years. He says something about how "young" and "beautiful" she looks, while his hands remain lovingly touching. She answers something about "taking [it] every morning," and how "he still treats me *in that very special way.*" Just as the ad is closing, she adds as a kind of aside, "Yes, and he takes [it] too."

The ad clearly plays upon aging and sexuality. Little reflection is necessary to draw out the human intimacies, the human anxieties, loneliness, and vulnerabilities that are here being manipulated for the purposes of hawking a product that is wholly impotent to fulfill the covert promises of the ad. This is but one example of thousands of such commercials which convert the private and intimate spaces of persons into the raw material of the public marketplace. This advertising goes on daily and mostly without protest—not even inner anger at the indignity of it all—as the lines of permissible trespass upon privacy remain without definition in the everyday world of business and commerce. We shall return to this in more detail in chapter three. For the moment it is enough to notice how passively we submit to this routine and sustained invasion of our communities of intimacy, an invasion that transforms our private lives into the public workshops of commercial interests.

So much for profit. Now what about public pacification?

Record prisons

Senator Thomas Eagleton of Missouri must have felt himself a doubly haunted man, not only by his medical dossier but, thanks to columnist Jack Anderson, by his driving records as well. This machine-retained, readily accessible, and in the latter case inaccurate, retention of his remote past, very nearly ruined his career. How much of this kind of record keeping is defensible? How much socially beneficial and necessary?

To be sure, every society has not only the right but also the positive obligation to protect itself and its constituent members. A helpless or ineffective government is *not* a viable alternative as we weigh the rights of individuals against the rights of society. By the same token, a society in which there is no effective "right to privacy" is not acceptable either. The task of striking a balance that is appropriate to a social order which aspires also to be a free and democratic order is nowhere better illustrated, and its present imbalance better documented, than in the area of *the rights of arrested persons.*

According to the FBI, law enforcement agencies make some 7.5 million arrests each year, excluding traffic offenses. Of these, 3.5 million are never prosecuted or have their charges dismissed. Add to this the fact that of the cases which eventually go to trial only 25 percent are found guilty, and you begin to get an idea of the size of the arrest-without-conviction issue. The probability, for example, of a black urban male being arrested at least once during his lifetime has been estimated as high as 90 percent. For white urban males the figure is 60 percent, and for all males it is 47 percent.

Unlike the conviction record, the arrest record is an illegitimate offspring of the criminal justice system, whose chief task, after all, is to separate the innocent from the guilty—to separate the simply arrested from the properly tried and convicted. This seems doubly the case when too often *both* types of records end up exacting the same human price. A recent study of New York area employment agencies indicated that fully 75 percent would not accept for referral an applicant with an arrest record even though *without conviction*. An estimated 56 percent of all states, 55 percent of all counties, and 77 percent of all cities ask on their civil service application forms whether an applicant has ever been arrested (not convicted). The unfairness of this punishment by arrest, this record prison, is illustrated by hundreds of thousands of wrecked lives less celebrated than Senator Eagleton, who was, after all, at least convicted of "speeding."

There is a further issue. That is the new demand of computer technology for a standard codification of data (as in the FBI's National Crime Information Center) with the resulting "de-refinement" of arrest records and their use. Professor Miller illustrates the concrete implications of this in the following hypothetical computer profile: "Arrested, June 1, 1962; disorderly conduct and criminal conspiracy; convicted, April 12, 1963; sentenced, May 21, 1963, six months." Who is it? A street rioter? A local mafioso with a friendly judge? A hardened and dangerous criminal needing society's careful tracking? Actually, it might well be your minister, priest, or rabbi who may have spent a summer out of his seminary training working in the South, registering black citizens to vote. As Miller concludes, the conviction "merely reflects the now-discredited judicial and law enforcement practices of a decade ago of inhibiting the exercise of constitutionally protected right. . . ." [23] After the anti-Vietnam protests of the late sixties, we have of course a whole new generation of these "suspects."

Evidently it is easier for a country to shed its discredited past than for an honorable citizen who stood his ground in that past to disengage his reputation from obsolete and out-of-context computerized arrest data. In fact this whole area is so chaotic in regard to privacy rights that Federal Judge Gesell in a recent celebrated case *(Menard* v. *Mitchell),* observing that the FBI "could not prevent improper dissemination and use of the material it supplies to hundreds of local agencies," concluded that *"the system is out of effective control."*

A criminal record system "out of control" that in effect convicts by arrest and incarcerates without benefit of trial hundreds of thousands in "record prisons" plainly needs correcting. Meanwhile, domestic security has become not simply a matter of legal arrest but of the use of law, sometimes quite illegally, to pacify political dissent. This is the message of *Watergate*, which to ignore is to ignore the future of freedom in America.

Suspect citizenship

Frank Donner, director of the American Civil Liberties Union's Project on Surveillance, speaks in a recent article of a "system of political intelligence, which is rapidly coalescing into a national network." One very chilling example of this kind of intelligence gathering at the local level has been found in Philadelphia. There the Civil Disobedience Unit of the police force has been active in covering all kinds of protest meetings, rallies, marches, and the like. The officers have become very familiar with the leaders of these demonstrations—their associates, family ties, techniques, and organizational affiliations. The police keep watch, take photographs, and make records of the events. Donner concludes that "we can no longer seriously doubt that the main purpose of such activity is political control of dissent. . . ."[24] The evidence indicates that the purpose is working.

Consider the Senate testimony of Jerome Weisner of Harvard University and former science advisor to President Kennedy. His comments (1971) on the governmental response to student activism of the sixties is sobering. In the late 1960s academia was in disorder and the government set out to drive the students back into quietude. In some cases Military Intelligence personnel were dispatched to maintain a systematic surveillance of campus activities. In others it was the FBI. Witness the following Bureau memo:

> Each office submit by airtel to reach Bureau by 12/4/70, a list of BSUs (Black Student Unions) and similar groups by name and school which are or will be subjects of preliminary inquiries. This program will include junior colleges and two-year colleges as well as four-year colleges. In connection with this program, there is a need for increased source coverage and we must develop network of discrete quality sources in a position to furnish required information.[25]

According to Dr. Weisner's testimony, such blanket governmental surveillance soon became known to the students, who responded somewhat like hungry rats who are compelled to cross an electrified wire grid to get a morsel of cheese: namely, with a phenomenon psychologists call "vacillation," a precursor to anxiety neurosis. Weisner concluded,

Many, many students are afraid to participate in political activities of various kinds which might attract them because of their concern about the consequences of having a record of such activities appear in a central file. They fear that at some future date, it might possibly cost them a job or at least make their clearance for a job difficult to obtain.[26]

If privacy is freedom to grow, freedom to experience and to control what others may know about oneself, then in many ways it is the first line of defense of other freedoms. It conditions the climate of public breathing space. The military or the FBI, by impinging upon the mental elbowroom of the students, whose range of activities is in turn necessarily narrowed by their psychological reaction to the presence of that surveillance, interfered not only with their privacy but also with their exercise of democratic freedom.

But even if this political dampening effect results, is such surveillance in fact illegal? After all, monitoring meetings, photographing persons in crowds, and collecting membership lists are hardly the kinds of conduct found in the past to be offensive to the Fourth Amendment. Privacy may be defined as having three necessary components: (1) a person's ideas or intellectual work product, (2) his private activities, and (3) his own "life space." Society has the right, so government has consistently claimed, to invade these privacies in order (1) to formulate public policy, (2) to fight crime, and (3) to protect national security. This governmental "need to know" has been used for many years to justify the activities of the Congressional Un-American Activities Committees and Committees on Internal Security. It led to the institution of "security checks" upon government employees that in turn gave impetus to the development of new methods of inquiry into interpersonal relationships, personality characteristics, emotional stability, sexual practice, recreational preferences, and a variety of other personal matters.

This same "need to know" led to the investigation in the name of national security of such notorious American "underworld figures" as Senator Adlai Stevenson III as well as nearly eight hundred other Illinois citizens by United States Army Intelligence agents. The army initially claimed that it investigated only those who had demonstrated a penchant for violence or criminal conduct. However, in face of proof that Stevenson and others were intelligence targets, the army conceded that "It was enough . . . that they opposed or did not actively support the Government's policy in Vietnam or that they disagreed with domestic policies of the Administration, or that they were in contact or sympathetic to people with such views."[27] Evidently, not only students but also more respectable types—indeed, almost anyone who is not simply a passive unit of social administration—risk the invasion of their personal privacy and political freedom.

If this description begins to sound more uncomfortably like 1984 than we are accustomed to, a far more ominous note is struck by the clearly *illegal* surveillance activities apparently OK'd by President Nixon and revealed to the Senate Watergate Committee by Presidential Counsel John Dean. I refer to the so-called "Huston Plan"—named for its author—by which the president gave his blessing to:

(1) intensified electronic surveillance of both domestic security threats and foreign diplomats;
(2) monitoring of American citizens using international communications facilities;
(3) increased legal "mail coverage" (exterior examination to determine sender, postmark, etc.) and relaxation of restrictions on illegal mail coverage (opening and reading);
(4) more informants on college campuses;
(5) lifting of restrictions on "surreptitious entry" [i.e., authorizing burglary];
(6) establishment of an Interagency Group on Domestic Intelligence and Internal Security, with representatives from the White House, the F.B.I., the C.I.A., the N.S.A., the D.I.A. and the three military counter-intelligence agencies.[28]

This approach reflects the virtual siegelike mentality of the White House, which viewed local dissenting citizens as "enemies" not just of their particular policies, but also of the United States. Such arrogance of office shows no understanding of or sympathy for the domestic ferment necessary to democracy. This attitude is at the very least a touchy and unsure paternalism.

We are told that the Huston Plan was later rescinded because of pressure from outside the White House. Still, someone out there was clearly "operational," not only with the well-known break-in of Dr. Ellsberg's psychiatrist, but also with the less publicized allegations of two defense lawyers and one defendant in the "Seattle 7" case who reported break-ins before, during, and just after their December, 1970, trial. Moreover, Senate investigators have been told that government agents were involved in other burglaries at defense offices during the trials of Philip Berrigan, the Chicago Weathermen, and the "Detroit 13."

All this evidence reveals a catastrophic withering of our constitutional protection against government interference with the privacy of our personal and public lives. We will do well to remember a 1969 Supreme Court decision *(Stanley* v. *Georgia)* in which it quoted favorably an earlier statement by Justice Brandeis. He stated that "the right to be let alone" by the government is "the most comprehensive of rights, and the right most valued by civilized men."[29] The Court concluded that "the right to be free, except in very limited circumstances, from unwarranted governmental intrusions into one's privacy" is fundamental.

Reversing Public and Private

Profit and the politics of pacification—together these constitute an impressive motive for the attack upon privacy of persons and groups. They argue a very different social logic from democratic participation, the logic of an administrative state which maximizes the advantages of the already well-advantaged while passing down propaganda to the many, and all at the price of the freedom and dignity of the individual. Which is to say, the current assault upon personal and associational privacy reflects more than the psychological anomalies of certain high government officials. It points to a more fundamental attack upon our traditional values. That challenge is the process by which the distribution of public goods and services is increasingly withdrawn into the private decision making of industrial-government hierarchies, administrative agencies, and behind-the-scenes "big deals."

Put simply, while we become more public and transparent as persons, the public world becomes more private, secretive, and monopolized as to power and advantages. Thus, those who speak both for personal privacy and for the *public's* "right to know" are not arguing at cross-purposes. They are seriously concerned about the business of preserving citizenship under the prevailing social conditions. We turn to an analysis of this in the next chapter.

2

The Ambitions of the Administrative State

> We both consider the people as our children, and love them with parental affection. But you love them as infants whom you are afraid to trust without nurses; and I as adults whom I freely leave to self-government.[1]
>
> —Thomas Jefferson,
> in a letter to Du Pont de Nemours

"I don't care who watches me; I have nothing to hide" seems at first an evenhanded and judicious response. It seems so, that is, until one notices that it represents a rather awesome reversal of the order of explanations traditional to a democracy. The right to watch over belongs first of all to the people against the governing authorities rather than the reverse. This order of affairs seems obvious enough if it is liberty that we are after.

Citizens and Clients

Perhaps I should say the right of the citizen *used to* seem obvious. For what is striking today is the deference and subservice of persons before those in governing authority. One wonders where our pride as free citizens has gone, that "they" should not first of all *have to explain themselves* to us; that the censorial power should come to reside in the government over the people. How did this change from citizen to client come about?

Bureaucracy and freedom

More than a hundred years ago Alexis de Tocqueville spoke of a gathering crisis he believed someday would threaten to undo our attempt at democratic civilization, "It is easy to foresee that the time is drawing near," he said,

> when man will be less and less able to produce, by himself alone, the commonest necessities of life. The task of the governing power will therefore perpetually increase, and its very effort will extend it every day. The more it stands in the place of associations, the more will individuals, losing the notion of combining together, require its assistance.[2]

Here de Tocqueville foresaw the growth of what we might call the administrative-welfare state and the increasing dependence of individuals upon its centralized system of social management. There is a closing in and totalizing of the context of everyday life, a loss of that intermediary network of vital interdependencies that pluralize the social landscape.

With the impoverishment of these middle structures the citizen is left in a new relationship to society. He is more alone. With reference to the basic necessities of life he finds himself ever more directly dependent upon the general political order. His voluntary associations play an increasingly marginal, almost recreational, role in his life. As a consequence he lives more "totally" within the administrative-welfare state, without the buffers once provided by middle level communities. Bureaucratic efficiency replaces neighborly good deeds. And bureaucratic efficiency requires that the client "be known" for accurate targeting of services.

In a recent exchange Judge David Bazelon of the Court of Appeals in Washington told of a case which illustrates the problems implicit in this need to know. A member of the board of directors of a Cooperative Health Information Center in Vermont, he is concerned about privacy of medical records. Yet to achieve reform in the financing and delivery of health care, sufficient data is required to monitor the quality of health services. He used the example of a recent survey which indicated marked disparities in tonsillectomy rates between various Vermont towns—varying from 20 to 50 percent. Either some areas are receiving less medical care than needed or there is overdoctoring going on, and, as the judge pointed out, "only adequate data can decide which."

We're not just citizens of the modern state; we are also its clients, who, to be serviced and protected, must be known. The "need to know" of public administrators is inseparable from our need for public care. The issue between privacy and well-performed social service is an issue of *proper balancing, not wholesale flight.*

It's too simple to damn bureaucracy and head for the woods. For one thing, most people can't afford to escape—especially poor people, elderly people, those with special handicaps, the disadvantaged who need special care, and others. Also, an examination of the recent career of privacy reveals that the industrial and bureaucratic state actually has advanced the development of human autonomy. The woods, we need remember, were never that private to begin with, not if you planned to survive, and village neighbors were always inordinately inquisitive.

The rise of urban industrial society at first greatly *expanded* the dimensions of both personal reserve and interpersonal intimacy. Such a society provided a vastly more stimulating environment as compared to the village. Village life was characterized by a concentration of energy, curiosity, and imagination. Each man "belonged" to his neighbor because of the constrictedness of the horizon of everyday attention. In the industrial city, places of residence and places of work become separate. People commute between a number of concrete life settings. It is not only more difficult to focus curiosity; there is simply more on scene to expand and divert attention. The affairs that draw our interest tend to be wider and more public than the people across the street. Meanwhile, at the level of everyday commingling there is a growth of formalism, of relative personal inattentiveness, a taken-for-granted fulfilling of social roles. All this happens precisely because our basic human needs connect us not to the workshop next door or the farmer's cart on the square, but to a bureaucratic system of human provision.

Sometimes we bemoan such "impersonality" without careful reflection. For living in a more formal and impersonal world makes possible a greater voluntarism in interpersonal relationships, and hence *a greater intensity of intimacy.* Bureaucracy makes space in the compact "world of watching neighbors" for freedom from routine self-disclosure, and so a new depth of interpersonal sharing is possible when freely timed and chosen. We "make friends" rather than inherit them.

All this of a positive nature happened as we have said, "at first." But as industrial society continued to develop toward maximizing efficiency and productivity, fundamental contradictions vis-à-vis human autonomy were forced to the surface. Managers of complex social systems became increasingly aware of the value of accurately predicting the behavior of their system-inhabitants. The desire to predict tended to dominate other values. As industrial societies grew more complex and structurally interdependent, effective power became ever more consolidated into systematic forms of interrelationship. There developed, in short, an elite at the center of society. Managers of complex industrial organizations and managers of social service networks found themselves with similar problems and so cultivated compatible perspectives upon reality.

These needs of "administration" brought upon the former impersonalism and open spaces of urban society a new compulsion—the need to know. Maximizing administrative efficiency required maximizing accurate prediction, and that meant bringing formerly secluded and open spaces of society under surveillance to make sure that nothing surprising or unplanned for came out of them. The era of testing, whether consumer appetite or voter preference, was born; and beyond testing came active management and then public pacification. Citizen autonomy has come into tension with client control.

Locating the problem

Still, this managerial mentality did not yet pose an insuperable threat to personal reserve and initiative. Bureaucratic administration is subject to the definition of its overall goal. Once defined, its internal mind set will seek to pursue that goal efficiently. But conceivably the goal might include a firm grasp on such democratic values as individual reserve and autonomy. Indeed, our final chapter will make concrete suggestions for precisely this. Such a *balancing of values* would simply represent the effective reminder that "the object" of social or commercial service is in turn "a subject"—a personal center of independent meaning and value. It is perfectly conceivable that governmental and industrial bureaucracies could recognize this human dignity and discipline their activities (or have them disciplined) to the end of preserving and even enhancing dignity.

While this positive effect is conceivable, it isn't happening. We will examine why in a moment. Notice in passing, however, that my analysis has carefully avoided any wholesale condemnation of bureaucracy. Rather, I have tried to drive the wedge of analysis not between persons and just any advanced industrial society but between individuals and *a system of basic inequality,* a system of the privatization of power. For the structure of inequality represents not only a trespass against personal dignity, and so indifference to personal privacy. It also actively seeks secrecy, to hide its stratagems of special advantage, and the pacification of public protest.

Privatizing Public Power

By "basic inequality" I do not intend that kind of natural inequality that inheres in us simply because we are born with different talents. Nor do I mean that inequality that is ours not perhaps as biological beings but as social ones—the inequality of social function and reward. In fact a degree of the latter I would affirm as probably socially necessary and in any case inevitable, although I think that Reinhold Niebuhr had the major part of truth in saying, "If superior abilities and services to society deserve special rewards it may be regarded as axiomatic that the rewards are always higher than the services warrant." [3]

By "basic inequality" I mean an interplay of social structures so as to form *a system of inequality,* a system from which individual escape tends only to disguise and so reinforce the system's overall logic. I do not refer to the formation of cultural elites or of social heirarchy, all of which again appears to me as inevitable, but *the general organization of society to return to a small minority inordinate and unjustifiable benefit.* I mean, therefore, the secreting and privatization of public power and the consequent evisceration of citizen consent.

The takeover

Ironically, the opportunity for the rapid expansion of this monopoly of advantage was first provided not by human ambition but by certain structural changes in the means of production. The economist John Kenneth Galbraith has referred to this as "the new industrial state." [4] What is new about this situation is the tremendous expansion in size of corporations and the dependence of the overall domestic economy upon their successful performance. With this rapid expansion in corporate size—including the unification of corporate ownership in conglomerates—management has become ever more exposed to the contingencies of time. Large outlays of capital are needed far in advance of any possible product marketing and return on investment. This means a high degree of exposure to market vicissitudes in between the making of plans and their fulfillment.

In response, management has sought ways of minimizing risk by extending relative control over the market. And this control can be effectively established only with the cooperation of the regulatory agencies of government. Thus, if Galbraith is correct, the very structure of modern industrial production, at least large-scale production, encourages a certain everyday passing back and forth between industry, corporate law, and government regulatory agencies. It produces a kind of symbiosis of the hierarchies, a behind-the-scenes fraternalism, which can be easily subverted for the sake of private advantage. The foundations thus were laid for a new and structurally far more comprehensive "Teapot Dome," a kind of corporate/government takeover of effective public power. It would be accomplished, clearly, only at the expense of a fundamental erosion of democratic control.

Still, we have said only that "the foundations were laid." The actual attempt to build upon these new possibilities leads our analysis beyond inherent developments in the structure of production to strategies of human ambition. We come, in short, upon the conscious development of a system of basic inequality whose end product has been a rather staggering concentration of social control. There is an impressive degree of unanimity amongst political scientists that precisely such a privatization of power is now well underway in our country. Its existence is the central lesson of "Watergate," far more important than the personal illegalities revealed there.

We may begin with the fact that modern electioneering is fantastically expensive. In 1972 Republican Hugh Scott of Pennsylvania, running against only token Democratic opposition, spent over one million dollars in his bid for Senate reelection. That same year Richard Nixon spent between fifty and fifty-five million dollars to retain the presidency. Politicians need of course to get the votes of the public, but in order to go public in the first place they must collect a good deal of private wealth.

Take the case of the $430,000 "contributed" to Nixon's campaign chest by the National Milk Producers Association. It was solicited by Herb Kalmbach, until Watergate fame the president's personal lawyer. The request for a contribution came shortly after the White House reversed a Department of Agriculture recommendation to lower milk price supports. The fact that the regulatory agency acted here in behalf of the public interest as against the interest of organized private producers—and so had to be reversed by the White House—is a hopeful sign. It points in the direction of needed reforms. Unfortunately, the relationship between the regulators and the regulated is often much more cozy, and they act in concert.

The ITT/Dita Beard affair is an example. Various antitrust laws are intended to be administered by the Justice Department to protect the public against corporate mergers which might monopolize the market. A friendly arrangement, however, was worked out between ITT President Robert Goheen and former Attorney General John Mitchell. ITT wanted to buy out the Hartford Insurance Company to get hold of its vast liquid assets. The attorney general was, as we know, dedicated to Mr. Nixon's reelection. Goheen offered a friendly $400,000 to underwrite expenses at the Republican National Convention in 1972. Shortly thereafter, the Justice Department—reversing the opinion of the Securities and Exchange Commission—handed down a most generous decision on the merger petition.

But this "I scratch your back and you scratch mine" attitude of administrative agencies and their administered clientele goes on more routinely not for political purpose but for private gain. Take the Russian wheat deal boondoggle. Enormous profits were involved. A government audit showed three hundred million dollars in federal subsidies alone. The deal was negotiated in secret by the White House and high officials in the Department of Agriculture. Advance knowledge would be of immense benefit to any grain corporation, which could then buy wheat from unsuspecting farmers at existing prices, knowing all the while that demand and thus price were about to skyrocket. Curiously, just such profits were realized by a few companies. And curiously, two top Department of Agriculture officials left government service a few weeks after the wheat sale was announced to accept board chairmanships of two of the large grain corporations. Very cozy, indeed!

This is but an example of what has caused political scientists to conclude that government administrative agencies administer public power mostly not for public benefit but for private gain. Citizen consent is expropriated by behind-the-scenes big deals.

Fictionalizing citizen consent

That government does things in secret to serve its own purposes rather than ours should come as no surprise in the post-Pentagon Papers era. Political scientist Hannah Arendt remarks that the most striking thing illustrated there is the massive "defactualization" of the political world. Questions of face, of reputation, the language of "scenarios" and "audiences" preoccupies the talk of the decision makers. The issue is not citizen consent but administrative manipulation of public opinion.[5] In fact Miss Arendt seems to distinguish herself by her sense of outrage. John Scharr, who is also outraged, points out that most social scientists today view "a polity not as a people with a culture seeking together the forms of order and action that will preserve and enhance that culture, but as a mass or collective that is made into a unit of control by propaganda."[6]

Many of those these days who professionally seek to explain us to ourselves urge us to become modern and behavioral— sophisticated fellow travelers of the new administrative state. The "sovereignty of the electorate" is not only a fiction, but also it is an inevitable fiction—perhaps even a happy one, so they say.

When voting is going on, that's not what's really going on at all. Voting has very little to do with citizen ratification or its refusal of a particular administration's use of public power. It has to do instead with "symbolic gratification," especially powerful symbolic "reassurance" in the face of "threat." Thomas Jefferson ("adults I freely leave to self-government," etc.) to the contrary, *paternalism* for many professionals seems to be the very heart and substance of politics.[7]

Well—perhaps. But as Du Pont de Nemours knew full well, it's mighty nice to think that way if you've got a corner on public profit. Undermining respect for citizenship and excusing it in the name of human nature lays the attitudinal foundation for a free-handed manipulation of public power for private benefit. Gentle cynicism concerning the adulthood of citizens serves (it seems) the purposes of the given game, its rules, and given rulers.

Wealth distribution

I am attempting to show that while the private world of the self is increasingly turned public, the public world upon which that self more and more depends is being secreted into closed decision-making processes of government and commercial elites. This is the result, not of bureaucratic necessity, as some would hold, but of the pursuit of human ambition and the bending of society to that purpose.

By relating the attack upon privacy and the rise of official secrecy to a monopolization of control, which is in no way structurally necessary, I want to indicate that *the cancer of control can be excised while preserving the human benefits of advanced industrialization.*

The privatizing of public power is nowhere more graphically documented than in the increasing concentration of the nation's wealth. Money is always power. But when politics is expensive and privately financed, then wealth becomes a privileged enclave of social control. Always the boss in business, money becomes boss in Washington as well. And the recent concentration of wealth has been phenomenal. In 1949, 1 percent of our people owned 21 percent of the total personal wealth. By 1969 that same 1 percent owned 34 percent of the total personal wealth. That is, in the last twenty years those at the top have *increased* their distance in front of the rest of us by better than 50 percent.

We are not so much a "middle-class" country today as a country of *wage earners and wealth owners.* And if you're one, then you're not and will not become the other. This state of affairs is demonstrated by the structure of our tax and estate laws. Its net effect has been to multiply the advantages of the already advantaged at the expense of those who live by paycheck. Witness the following chart. It shows the percentage of yearly incomes in various brackets derived from "wage" and from "property and business" (interest, dividends, rents, ownership, etc.).

COMPOSITION OF INCOME, 1962[8]

Income	Wages and Salaries	Property and Business
0-2,999	41%	14%
3-4,999	72	13
5-7,499	84	11
7,5-9,999	85	12
10-14,999	84	14
15-24,999	78	20
25-49,999**	47**	51**
50-99,999	38	61
100,000+	17	82

Note the sharp break that comes (**) at about $25,000 ($30,000 today, due to inflation), the sudden and dramatic movement out of wage income over into property income. The reason is obvious. Taxation covers 95 percent of wages and salaries, while on property it covers only 65 percent and on farm income 37 percent. Capital-gains tax (on stocks), for example, averages only 50 percent of that on wages. Then there are tax-free municipal bonds, tax write-offs for business depreciation on loss or reinvestment, farm and oil subsidies, income-hiding stock options and expense accounts, company-provided cars, housing, and even vacations disguised as "business expenses." A single statistic sums up the whole picture: in 1971 a family earning $50,000 paid the same percentage of their income in taxes as those earning $5,000.

The break point from wage to wealth comes around $30,000 today. Since less than 3 percent of us make that much, just where does that leave the rest of us? Members of the powerless majority! Why do we take it?

The American Dream

Why *do* we take it? Is it because we despair of changing the situation? No, our willingness to go along has more to do, I think, with the way we live so often by a dream of reality rather than by reality. It has to do with human hope and meaning.

Public myths and public realities

We become citizens of a nation not so much by territory or birth but by "inhabiting" its myths of social meaning. Karl Mannheim says:

> We belong to a group not only because we are born into it, not merely because we profess to belong to it, nor finally because we give it our loyalty and allegiance, but primarily because we see the world and certain things in the world the way it does (i.e., in terms of the meanings of the group in question).[9]

We are deeply exposed as persons to these myths of public significance simply because we are people, poorly equipped by instinct, who, without a map, are lost. We use these myths to tell ourselves "what's going on," why "it's all worthwhile," and why we should get up when the alarm goes off. Thus, a state becomes *our state* by our common acceptance and practice of its myths of social meaning which "make sense" out of the time we spend there. How so for us Americans?

Unless I am mistaken, we Americans make our pledge of allegiance by a joint participation in *three central myths* of social meaning. These are "upward mobility," "the Good Life," and "freedom of opportunity."

For example, when we say that we're "middle class," we label ourselves as those who are "in-between"—those we envy and seek to emulate (above) and those we fear and flee from (below). This use of terminology is a highly political way of speaking which consolidates the given system of advantages by putting the majority at the service of the minority. But this "life in the middle" becomes a "respectable" place to live only as it always holds out the hope of passing beyond itself toward something better, as it has *upward mobility*. Since the actual distribution of wealth has been toward greater concentration, the dream of "moving up" has been sustained by the reality of an expanding gross national product. It's not the percentage piece of the pie that's getting bigger; it's the pie itself that is growing larger.

This rapid increase in overall economic activity has had two by-products. As inhabitants of this super-heated system, we have had to be "wired" ever more thoroughly as top-performing consumers. We will study this effect in more detail in the next chapter. Briefly, the effect is achieved with the use of psychological hard-sell advertising and the way in which the needs and vulnerabilities of our "insides" are converted into the raw material of rapid-pace buying and selling. A second by-product of the American system of myths and realities is the endless race for success, for "the Good Life."

We are, we are told, an "affluent" people, which is a bit curious given the statistics. In 1971 the average American family made just over $10,000. That same year, the Bureau of Labor Statistics projected an "Intermediate Level of Living" budget for a mythical urban family of four. Beginning with a salary of $10,971, or $9,186 after taxes and social security, the budget breakdown then looks like this:

Food: $50 a week, including every restaurant lunch and stadium hotdog.

Housing: $219 a month for all expenses—mortgage, utilities, furniture, house repair.

Medical: $612 a year, which must cover health insurance—about $460—all medicines, dental care, and so on.

Transportation: $964 a year, including car payments, gasoline, repairs, and insurance.

Clothing and personal care: $1,196 a year for clothes, shoes, makeup, hair care, etc.

$563 a year to cover life insurance, union dues, Christmas presents and charities.

$684 a year for liquor, tobacco, TV and radio and records, books, newspapers, school supplies, vacations, and toys.[10]

That's the life-style of a better-than-average American family. Is it a picture of affluence or more like end-of-the-month panic and supermarket defeat?

And consider how average families put this package together in the first place. The *New York Times* of November 18, 1968, reported the following income statistics (the figures covered white families only). The largest group—25.1% of the total white population—received between $7,000 and $9,999 per year. But to achieve this level, 56.1% of the families in this group had to have "two or more wage earners." At the $10,000 to $12,000 level, 66.9% of the families were there only on the basis of a second or third wage; and in the $12,000 to $15,000 bracket, these two- or three-wage families numbered 75.3%.[11] Not massive middle-class affluence but massive middle-class moonlighting is what these figures show. And they don't include the traffic patterns of black families trying to make it. Is this "the Good Life"? With the father holding down two jobs and/or the mother working, with the juggling of their family lives for the sake of balancing even modest family budgets, is it any wonder that many divorces occur because of "problems over money"?

Well, what would you have us do? If we don't believe in "middle" and "mobile" and "making it," what are we to believe in? We have to make sense of it all somehow, explain to ourselves why it's been worthwile. No one's life deserves a trifling summary. "Making it" is a matter for joking only among those who have forgotten the indignities visited upon the person lost in the middle and prey to haunting self-doubts. Is it any surprise that many of us feel that for all our running we get further behind each year? And in the end we wonder why life isn't a little better. Unfortunately, we usually blame ourselves and so ratify our own defeat.

The defeat of public anger

We live, they say, in "a land of opportunity." In New York harbor a statue faces across the ocean with the message: "Send me your tired, your poor . . . I lift my lamp beside the Golden Door."

An honorable intention, the thing that made our land the homeland of so many human dreams. But if taken as reality rather than unfinished task, the expression becomes psychologically devastating.

If we live in a "land of opportunity," and then have nothing for which to feel grateful, we haven't made it; and if we haven't made it, then we're "failures." Here the idea of freedom of opportunity shows its darker side. That we have (supposedly) "equal opportunity" in a land of opportunity leads to a devastating blow when we attempt to judge what we have done with this opportunity. Grateful we had better be! Or the fault lies with us, and there is a bottomless attack of the self upon its own self-esteem.

In the fascinating book *The Hidden Injuries of Class,* Richard Sennett and Jonathan Cobb document the social psychology that fuels the American Dream even as it consolidates American realities.[12] In a series of in-depth interviews with middle and lower middle-class workers they discovered two pervasive attitudes by which the workers interpreted their lives. One is *self-accusation.* They see themselves as "failures" and by their own fault (what else in a land of opportunity?). "Look," said one of them, "it's nobody's fault but mine I got stuck where I am." The sense of frustration and anger, which under the other circumstances might be directed against the external system of inequality, is targeted here inward against the self's sense of personal worth.

The second is *self-sacrifice.* Many of the parents saw their lives of deprivation as making sense because "we did it for the kids." The psychological impact of this elemental ambivalence—"I'm a failure, but you should love me because I did it all for you"— simply passes on the wound of status from one generation to the next. This attitude is reflected in the authoritarian way of raising children. Parents often view themselves not as models to be followed but as warnings. Suspecting their own competence and worth, they lack a fundamental trust in the competence of their offspring. Their kids aren't "born" winners, but with careful watching they might be made into winners. As one worker put it, "I haven't got it up here, but my kids are smart. *I make 'em that way.*" It's inevitable that the children pick up the covert signal, the suspicion of mediocre stock; and so the family story told between generations cripples rather than vitalizes its members.

In debt and owing the system everything we own, secretly

accusing ourselves as "failures" while outwardly practicing a pathetic gratitude, running the endless race, and trying to keep up face and arguing with each other about money, forlornly wishing the kids showed more respect—we fuel the American Dream too often with ourselves. We defeat our public anger by turning it into a private rancor of the self against itself and its own.

We have been talking about the reversal of public and private realms of reality—here is its starkest result. As persons we take it out against our own insides in the name of the myths of public meaning. Our personal inner space becomes a kind of colonial territory to the external system of social explanation and reward. The issue, then, is whether we will uphold the rights of our "insides" against the "outside," whether we will insist upon our dignity and esteem as selves over against the way the deck is stacked; or whether we will accept the sovereignty of the dealer over the dealt with. Some psychologists are persuaded there is no choice. The outside *is* the reality; the inside its passive reflection.

"Beyond Freedom and Dignity"?

In the administrative state, politics—the public ferment of citizen participation—is reduced to the manipulations of executive control, a control exercised for the benefit of the fortunate few. An arrogance of office develops which looks upon the political order as a mass held together by public opinion management, an "object" of propaganda. "Subjectivity" is denied, "personhood" counted a mistaken perception for a unit of behavior in a system of public control, "government of the people" the nostalgia of a more sentimental era. All this is given a certain intellectual credence by some modern interpretations of man. For example, consider B. F. Skinner's *Beyond Freedom and Dignity*.

I should begin, I suppose, by admitting that some people may feel I treat Skinner unfairly. He is a scientist after all. His methods of operant conditioning have proved not only reliable but also of enormous benefit in the training of retarded or mentally ill persons. None of this do I wish to deny. But with this recent book he enters upon society-wide prescription and needs to be judged in that context.

Professor Skinner thinks of himself as addressing his remarks to one kind of situation—mankind pressed against the wall of species survival. I see him speaking to quite another. I judge his argument in the context of the reversal of public and private realms of reality, and the social function of the humiliation of the person in pacifying inhabitants of the administrative state. Skinner thinks of himself as providing advice for the future; I see his explanations as reflecting the public realities of the present. As I, he, too, wants a more humane society. But I think he provides ideological justification for the established one. How so?

Professor Skinner views himself as offering advice to a world of unprecedented crisis. He begins his book speaking about "the terrifying problems that face us in the world today" where "things grow steadily worse." It is a time for radical action, "or all is lost." And the action needed is no less than a "technology of behavior." The old, "soft" forms of guiding human action must be replaced by a more total management.[13]

The language of freedom and dignity is part of this old view. It attributes human behavior to "indwelling agents" like "wills, impulses, feelings, purposes . . . intentions, aims and goals." It reflects the idea of an "inner" or "autonomous" man to whom appeals are directed, arguments presented, choices sought and urged. Skinner concludes that the time for discarding these sentimentalities is upon us. "If (our culture) continues to take freedom and dignity, rather than its own survival, as its principal value, then it is possible that some other culture will make a greater contribution to the future." [14]

What the times require, he claims, behavioral science now can offer. Human action can be studied and, more importantly, managed as a physical system in which "behavior is shaped and maintained by its consequences." The central idea is simple enough. "Behavior which operates upon the environment to produce consequences ['operant' behavior] can be studied by arranging environments in which specific consequences are contingent upon it." [15] Put briefly, control the "outside" and you control the "inside." A technology of human behavior thus becomes available to those trained in the administration of public environments. The inner space of persons is presented as naturally passive, a kind of empty space through which the management of external worlds can, with sufficient expertise, pass undisturbed. Everything is—or should be—planned, foreseen. The world can be saved from individual pride and caprice.

This humiliation of inner man is presented as all to human

benefit. Beyond freedom and dignity is also beyond personal praise or guilt. The times call for a beneficent programming of pleasantries. "Our task," as the professor says, "is not to encourage moral struggle or to build or demonstrate inner virtues. It is to make life less punishing...."[16] A fatherly benevolence replaces the inaccuracies and time-consuming inefficiencies, the sometimes costly personal sacrifice, of public debate in the arena of citizen advice and consent. Executive design is the reality which for these many centuries has lain hidden behind the fictions of a "private self"—an inflated self-estimate our threatened culture can no longer afford. The answer is, as you can see, not only a necessary but a pleasant therapy.

Now I want to pose three criticisms to Professor Skinner's argument which both summarize the issues of the present chapter and move us toward the next. *First,* I question his dismissal of "argument" and "explanation" as instruments for effecting human behavior. Skinner is caught in the obvious contradiction thereby of *arguing* for the abolition of argument. Clearly, his book is nothing but the presentation of an explanation—explaining behavior in its relationship to explanation and to environment. And just as clearly he means to modify our behavior thereby: making us less defensive about behavioral modification techniques, altering the priorities of federal support in psychological research, and so on. Moreover, Skinner has no "place" to present his case except to that inner man whose importance he has already denied, that is, he appeals to the judgment of the intellect concerning the logic and force of his arguments as against contrary evidence. By denying the importance to behavior of what he calls "mentalistic explanations," Skinner seems to reduce his years of teaching, writing, and seeking explanatory clarity to a nullity. Surely, he does not intend this effect and has overspoken his case.

Moreover, by undermining the force of explanation, of truth seeking and truth saying, Skinner lends support to that political view which interprets public discourse as nothing more than emotional motivators ("threats," "reassurances," etc.) directed from the leaders toward the led, as *by nature* propaganda. You can see how this view hollows out and fictionalizes the relationship between public officials and the citizen. Public communication becomes a matter not of serious inquiry into the shape and evolution of our common culture, but a question of performance, of image marketing. After Watergate, we may have second thoughts about such modernisms.

Second, Professor Skinner's attack upon inner space as irrelevant, his reduction of man's "insides" to a status of indifference, parallels the social psychology that fuels the established system of American inequality. The humiliation of inner space (the self accusing itself as a failure, etc.) and its surrender before the imposition of the myths of public meaning—a process which consolidates society in its given distribution of benefits—is here further consolidated by Skinner's removal of grounds for possible complaint. If he is correct, there is literally "no place" where man can turn back against his social conditionings, and so de-program himself for a new project of social construction. His inner self is lost and adrift in a public world.

Yet, something like cultural de-programming seems implicit in Skinner's general thesis. He can argue, for example, that "Man himself may be controlled by his environment but it is an environment which is almost wholly of his own making." [17] Yet, because he gives all the behavioral power to the "outsides" as against man's inner self, Skinner has no way of breaking out of the circle ("the man that man has made is the product of the culture man has devised" [18]) into something new.

In looking for a place of social leverage—I repeat, he does not explain theoretically how such a place exists—Skinner turns away from democratic procedures of guiding culture to elite models of social control. "The next step," he says, "is not to free men from control but to analyze and change the kinds of control to which they are exposed." [19] He transfers (uncritically) the clinical setting onto the political order and in the process reproduces the citizen as a "recipient" of behavior therapy, an "object" of behavioral management. [20]

Skinner does not seem to be aware of the possibility of educating the public in techniques of behavior control in order to heighten their awareness of and so gain reverse leverage against the ambitions of the controllers. He looks instead to the "professionalization" of environmental managers. The reason for this has to do with our first criticism. Skinner has already emptied out (to his own mind) the public significance of things like mind, consciousness, purpose, and so on. As a result, he is caught in a behavioral "loop" where the few already in charge are the only subjects worthy for the educators to bother educating. His model of society is essentially paternalistic, gratifying to the established hierarchies.

This brings me to my *third* criticism. Skinner, I think, misreads the signs of the times. In the name of survival he is willing to give away a good many human rights, the surrender of which in retrospect may prove to have been unnecessary, but once given over, enormously difficult to get back. For example, he argues against freedom and dignity, against a sense of personal regard and esteem, in favor of a proper humility. But this is a humility before social controllers who may have our species survival less on their minds than the survival of their own inordinate advantages. What if the signs of the times point to the ambitions of the administrative state and a system of basic inequality? In offering public prescription, Professor Skinner has stepped out of the relatively uncontroversial area of modifying, let us say, the incontinent behavior of retarded or brain-damaged persons. He has exposed himself to responsibility for reading correctly just "where we are" as a society, and into whose service his words are likely to be pressed. To my view, he has failed this task by failing to grasp adequately the power and profit realities of contemporary America.

Finally, this whole matter of "survival" seems to touch Skinner in a peculiarly deep and revealing way. Witness:

> The individualist has a special reason to fear death, engineered not by a religion but by the literatures of freedom and dignity. It is the prospect of personal annihilation. The individualist can find no solace in reflecting upon any contribution which will survive him.[21]

Death requires solace for Skinner, too, only after the fashion of cultural contribution. But what is it that needs such consoling? Surely not the outer world of environment, whose dreaming pleasantries can only be disturbed by this remembrance of lost gratitudes. No, it is the inner self, conscious of its fleeting moment of vitality, its waning grasp on any claim to recognition. It is this private self and its estimate of its own self-worth that needs consoling as it watches the future turn away in order to be "its own" rather than ours. This perpetual "ongoingness" of all "outer spaces" reminds us of how much in the end we are indeed *our own*—a subject we will return to in chapter 5.

Sociologist Amitai Etzioni of Columbia University is aware of man's social nature—"to be is to be social," he says. Yet, in a peculiarly happy phrase he takes this insight a different direction from Professor Skinner. He speaks of "the active society," of consciousness, commitment, and power.

> Without *consciousness*, the collective actor is unaware of his identity, his being acted upon, his ability to act, and his power; he is passive, like a sleeping giant. Without *commitment* to a purpose, action lacks direction and merely drifts. Without *power*, the most incisive and sharply focused awareness or the firmest commitment will not yield more action than a derailed train. *To be active is to be aware, committed, and potent.*[22]

To the extent *the ambitions of the administrative state* name our public reality today, we will do well to build up the tools of the active life: the consciousness, commitment, and power of persons, and the privacy of their associations of common loyalty. The next two chapters will deal with these issues.

3

Sustaining
Inner Space

> The sadist cannot stand the separation of the public and the private; nor can he grant to others the mystery of their personality, the validity of their inner self. . . . in order for reality to be convincing, in order for him to feel his maximum powers, he wants the world to be peopled with concrete manipulatable objects, with objects that do not have any elusive insides.[1]
>
> —Ernest Becker

Privacy implies an inner world, a self-space which is real, an invasion of which is a real invasion, a place we prize and preserve before others. Privacy, then, is a quality of our inter-human or transactional lives. It is less "being alone" than enjoying the right to determine when and how much of oneself is to be known by others. Intimacy is not the opposite of privacy. *Intimacy is the sharing of privacies.* The opposite of privacy is emptiness, resentment, or trivialization of inner space,[2] making our business everybody else's, or having it made such. Our task now becomes to establish with greater clarity the status of this inner space.

The Ego and Its World

How can we understand that we hold our place in reality as *self-conscious* creatures instead of simply organic and unaware? A table simply is what it is, at rest within itself. But we both are where we are and at the same moment approach ourselves from outside. We "take note of ourselves," become "aware of who we are." We turn back upon the place we hold and in some curious way from beyond it say "I." To so speak, is, you can see, an astonishingly lonely echo in a world of tables and chairs.

There's no doubt about it. "I" is a prideful word. It is a word full of self-esteem, full of boldness over against the internal slumbering and quiescence of the rest of the planet's creatures. Perhaps it's because they carry their world with them, like a snail and its shell, while man emerges out of an information gap. That is, other animals are energized and directed by an instinctual encoding, while we must *tell* ourselves what we need to know in order to survive. Indeed, we must persuade ourselves to listen. For we lack an internal conviction of reality, automatic animal persuasion. In a marvelously turned phrase anthropologist Ernest Becker has caught the vision of this. "Man," he says, "became man in *a total celebration of himself.*"[3]

"The lower animals are bound," Becker points out, "by instantaneous reactivity to a world of sensation." They remain "beds of sensation without a delaying, central control."[4] Man, on the other hand, takes his rise as a kind of rebel. He holds himself back from automatic reactivity. He refuses the world's immediacy. This sense of apartness we may call ego. Ego signals a new kind of freedom. It permits the organism to wait and to delay its response. As Becker says, it "creates time by 'binding' it; that is, the individual gives the world of events a fixed point of self reference."[5] You can see how exposed this makes us, this "I" that sticks out in an otherwise slumbering eternity of undisturbed stimulus and response. Ego is a kind of *proud and embarrassed privacy,* nourishing itself on a precarious celebration of its right to be this way.

But what is the *process* by which this "I" comes into being? Answering this question was the important contribution to our self-understanding by George Herbert Mead. He puzzled over man's capacity to unfold distances from his own immediacy. The very word "self," Mead saw, implied *reflexivity,* a capacity to depart undisturbed self-unity and so approach and take note of oneself from a distance. He concluded that all this became possible only because man is profoundly *social.* He argued:

The self, as that which can be an object to itself, is essentially a social structure, and it arises in social experience. After a self has arisen, it in a certain sense provides for its social experiences, and so we can conceive of an absolutely solitary self. But it is impossible to conceive of a self arising outside of social experience.[6]

Put simply, we view ourselves as "self" only because we have first *been viewed*. We can look back upon ourselves because we've first been looked upon. It is the attitude of others that provides this distance from our own immediacy. We come to ourselves *from outside in*.

Humanity is incubated in this very peculiar way. A baby, for example, randomly gestures (gurgles, smiles, reaches out, etc.) toward a "significant other" (Harry Stack Sullivan called it the "mothering figure"). The baby does not *know* the meaning of its gestures until that meaning is assigned to it by the response of the other. Only then does the baby's gesture become "known," emerge with distinctness out of random spontaneity and so become *useful*—literally, use-able. By means of these now "meaningful" gestures the baby begins to communicate its needs and wants. It begins to gain some control over its utter dependency, some distance from its overwhelming surroundings. It begins, in short, to assert itself *from inside out,* to make the world "out there" more responsive to its "in here."

This realization introduces us to one of the deepest ironies of our existence. The child begins to establish himself as an object of others *before* he becomes an executive subject. He begins not as a bold privacy externalizing itself, but as "a looking-glass self," a being absorbed in its *performance.* As a result, he is easily humiliated. As social creatures we entrust our "face" to others. How we approach and enjoy, but also how we distance and defend ourselves becomes crucial.[7]

Every society devises elaborate rituals for regulating the reciprocal performances of selves and for protecting the discreetness of self-space. The sense of the appropriate—how close, for example, people should stand in conversing with another; or the rituals of deference, those who must attend closely upon the other, or those whose status requires of them a certain indifference, an "oh, yes, my dear" as we look over the other person's shoulder— all of this must be precisely coordinated if a society is to keep from stumbling over itself. Indeed, we label severe incapacity in proper social performance "mental illness." A manic, for example, is one who after watching the conviviality of a well-performed scene of one person offering another a cigarette, falls all over himself showering a stranger with dozens of cigarettes, cigars, and assorted broad grins. We confine such persons to asylums, which, as Erving

Goffman saw, are "forcing houses" for changing persons to perform our play, to *act as expected*. Goffman calls them *total institutions*, where the profanation of self, the invasion of inner space, is a matter of routine therapy. Such therapy is clearly an effective way to break a person.[8]

We are creatures, then, who have both insides and outsides. We're a privacy and a performance, an "I am"/"what do you think of me?" dialectic. In this polarity of boldness and shyness the rights of personal reserve become crucial as a place to seclude ourselves from persistent exposure. Personal reserve lets us orchestrate, self-direct, so to say, our own disclosures. It is a way of maintaining ownership of oneself, of asserting the "I" over against engulfment in the social "me." Privacy builds up a sense of personal significance, of individual power and effectiveness. It is an indispensable tool in the active life and in the active society. Becker says it well: "Secrets and silences make life more real: the individual, self-absorbed and inwardly musing, taking himself very seriously, radiates a contagious aura: the tacit communication that the serious and the meaningful *exist*."[9] Still, it's not easy. Many want to use our insides against us and so bend our performance to their purpose.

Humiliation

Humiliation is the invasion of our inner silences and self-space to render us docile to the interests of others. It is an attack upon our dignity and reserve as persons. We may analyze it under three subtopics: (1) trivializing; (2) stigmatizing; and (3) degradation.

Trivializing

One of the places we seem most exposed to this kind of undermining is where we are most consistently visible, and in that sense consistently available to others: namely, our *body*. The problem, as the philosopher Jean-Paul Sartre saw it, is that we both *are* bodies and *have* bodies. That we *are* bodies is evident from the fact that we are somewhere-creatures, not everywhere-beings. We are locatable. We inhabit our place in reality as particularities, caught and held fast by our bodies. But even at the same moment we also *have* bodies. We can watch ourselves being watched, make judgments about how we are seen or touched. We are doubly exposed: both to the other's eyes, and to the fact that we can watch those eyes watching us. That's why Sartre found "body" such a burden. "I keep getting stolen from myself by the other person's eyes," he exclaimed![10]

This insight relates with particular weight in our culture to the woman. Her social role has been to be *the watched*. In a peculiar way she is trapped in her body—awaiting there her "recognition." She becomes an outside whose insides are given content and meaning only through others. Man, with his eyes, confers her place in reality. The Genesis creation story (written by men!) has Adam actively recognizing Eve—"flesh of my flesh, etc."—while she passively submits to his sovereign gaze. God doesn't even talk to her until after the world has been set up and she safely married off. And when at last "He" does speak, the first thing he tells her is that she should be ashamed. It's a nice bit of cultural insight; for *to be* as "one who is seen" is in a sense to be perpetually embarrassed, perpetually watching oneself being watched. All this, Sartre saw, is a subtle kind of combat. And in it *our bodies become the ammunition of the other*.

This is one of commercial advertising's most beloved insights. Knowing little of modesty, advertising is adept at using our outsides to domesticate our insides, taming us to its business purposes. In doing so it *trivializes* our estimate of our inner space, rendering us exposed and malleable, a kind of commercial workshop, sometimes in the name of liberation. Witness an advertisement for *Glamour* magazine that ran under the title "New Body Language." Already the irony appears since it is woman's traditional enslavement to be forced to "speak" with her body. It's supposedly what she has mostly to say. The ad continues:

> New Body Language—Glamour defines it. Tells a new generation of free-thinking young women how it's communicated. In clothes and in posture. In what they wear and what they bare. The magazine records the Breakaway Girl's total acceptance of her body and sex. Neither flaunting it nor hiding it. It previews the new liberation of mind, body and fashion that will shape the decade of the Seventies.[11]

This is accompanied by a full-page picture of a young woman wearing jeans, hands in her pockets, posture relaxed, at ease, sweater cut short to reveal a bold and delicious navel. The face is directly forward, an expression of both availability and in-difference, of accomplished worldliness and whimsy—a kind of invulnerability.

Now the first thing to note is that the ad is an *obvious lie*. It says it's about free-thinking young women and their liberation. But if women became truly free-thinking, they would also become unmanipulable to the fashion makers, and *Glamour* and its many companions would immediately go out of business. No, the advertisement is about *selling,* not liberation. It's about using a woman's outside to manipulate and manage her inside—her view of herself, her sense of personal worth, her search for security—and thus her *commodity choice.* The place of attack is the body: its irreducible shyness, its persistent exposure before the assessing eyes of others. The implied promise is body competence ("total acceptance of her body and sex"), an "I" freed to enjoy its executive powers, to self-sufficiency. But the psychodynamics of the ad depend upon—*in fact deepen*—precisely the opposite: a woman's caughtness in the open-ended vulnerability of her body presentation. It's a picture, I submit, not of sexual liberation but of the commercial exploitation of our culturally induced sex roles—an "I" trapped within its social "me." The result is an inward trivialization. *We learn our world as commercial objects rather than personal subjects.* It's a remarkably honest statement of how our society wants us to be.

I've spoken of the "open-ended vulnerability of body presentation" to indicate that we never reach a final solution about living with our bodies. Like food or clothing or warmth in winter our bodies remain a continuing anxiety. As such our bodies prove especially fit instruments for the service of our society's structural needs. We have noted, for example, that one of the consequences of our system of inequality—and the rapid expansion of the gross national product used to disguise it—is the social need to "wire" us aggressively as high-performance consumers. Open-ended vulnerabilities present an open-ended opportunity for sustained commercial advantage. Business taps into hoped-for satisfactions that remain, and by nature must remain, endlessly unsatisfied, inner fuel for the ever expanding external market. Our human insecurities and longings are redirected from the precariousness of persons to the ownership of products. In the *Glamour* ad, for example, our longing for body approval is carried not to another person—which is the only place of real confirmation—but to the possession of certain commodities (clothes, makeup). Some of the most lovely ways in which we depend upon each other for gentle handling are used thereby to strengthen the commercial system while leaving us more alone before each other. This wholesale transvaluation of persons and products should be embarrassing. But it goes on without evident protest.

This same kind of intense wiring of persons to gain commercial advantage can be seen at work in our dependence as individuals upon the myths of public meaning. We've analyzed in a previous chapter the pacification function of working class *self-accusation* ("failure," etc.). We can add now the commercial debasement of the average man's *hopes*. This is illustrated in a recent advertisement for the Pennsylvania State Lottery. There is a picture of an elderly male, broadly grinning and holding a winning ticket. "Want to share in the secret of the winner's success?" asks the ad. "It's really very simple: just make sure you buy your 50¢ Lottery ticket this week and every week. Then hope for Lady Luck to smile on you too!" A closer look at the picture reveals that the smile is mostly toothless, the face timeworn and tired, the suit too big, and the shirt rumpled. It's the picture, in short, of a hard life mostly over, a life that *didn't* "make it," unable to afford dental care or even a decent suit. Still, there's hope—"Lady Luck!"

Or think of all those television quiz shows pumping hour after hour into America's kitchens—"The Price Is Right," "Let's Make a Deal." Think of the trumped-up suspense, the hushed moment of truth, the squeals of delight—"a new bedroom set"—or the sad wisdom of afterthought—"I shouldn't have made the bet." Main-Line Americana, landing the once-in-a-lifetime "Big Deal," Willy Loman's Uncle Ben (in *Death of a Salesman*) walking into Africa as a young man and coming out wealthy! It's the Great American Dream.

Thus the public myth of making it, combined with the locked-in structures of actual advantage—all this explosive social contradiction is *harmlessly vented* into a two-dollar racetrack bet, the great lottery-ticket hope, or vicarious TV triumphs and tragedies. To put it simply, advertising has little to gain from directing our attention to the system of inequality in America as the place to apply our emotional energy. But the ad game does do a lot of gaining by skillfully playing upon the myths of public meaning and the fact that as persons we get caught and exposed in them. Perhaps that new suit of clothes, that new car, that new suburb, even that new love affair will put me over the top—a WINNER at last!

If it's true, as the Bible says, that without vision the people perish, it's also true that people get defeated by the wrong vision, by misplaced hopes. In America today we are encouraged to fasten our hopes upon the private accumulation of products, while the structure of established advantages remains deprived of emotional attention or energy. One by one we dream of the "Big Break," while society presents itself as closed and finished. So we play out our hopes by the established public myths, our inner self-estimate fueling the system's hold on us. Our privacies have become public raw material.

Whether body image or myths of public meaning, we will want, I should think, to turn this process around: making the social system an instrument of our humanity, not instrumentalizing our humanity to service the system. The first step, as Professor Etzioni earlier reminded us, is to become *conscious,* to become *aware,* to thrust the boldness of the questioning "I" over against the internal slumbering of the social "me." We *are* not trivial. But in a society that practices a kind of commercial shamelessness upon us, we can come to think of ourselves that way, as persons who have nothing important to say and so should keep still.

Stigmatizing

There are many ways to illustrate the stigmatizing process, from adolescents calling one another "chicken" to the massive IQ labeling and tracking system which so indelibly marks our lives. However, the most interesting issues of privacy and humiliation arise in connection with mental illness. In an intriguing argument, the psychiatrist Thomas Szasz *(The Myth of Mental Illness)* holds that designating deviant behavior as sickness is a "myth" or metaphor that has outlived its usefulness.[12] Nevertheless, it is a myth still very much in practice.

To suffer from mental or emotional distress is bad enough. It's worse to get caught at it and be officially labeled "mentally ill." You are reduced thereby to the status of a peculiar kind of "patient"—a patient who cannot be trusted as responsible for himself. You are, quite precisely, taken out of your own hands and left dependent and exposed. This humiliation is outwardly symbolized by the deprivation of normal civil rights. Labeled mentally ill, the citizen may be stripped of his property, dismissed from his job, deprived of his right to drive, denied his right to enter into contracts and to make or remake wills, and all too often committed to what society euphemistically calls hospitals but which for many are a kind of prison or final port of entry this side of a forgotten death. Not even the suspected or convicted felon suffers the indignities visited upon the mentally ill. The criminal is presumed at least to be an adult, a subject for caution, not ridicule.

To be wealthy and labeled "mentally ill" is to be stigmatized. To be poor and mentally distressed is to be abandoned. In the latter case the limited protection of privacy offered by the private therapist is lost in that exposure system which is the everyday routine of publicly supervised programs of mental care. A person may find himself, for example, using a community mental-health program where consultation and treatment must, under federal or state regulations, identify the names of their clients and the nature of the services rendered in order to remain eligible for public funding. Fed into the government data network, the person loses all control over this highly personal and potentially very damaging information. Once "well," he remains haunted by the ghost of his previous humiliation.

Beyond this initial loss of face, which is required as a kind of entrance fee, there is the further exposure of institutional living and therapy. The mental patient is routinely presented as an object of curiosity to such visiting luminaries as state legislators, crusading politicians, college students, bureaucrats of various types (most of them not therapeutic but administrative), and a variety of public persons whose sympathy is thought valuable by the hospital administrators. "The odd," after all, have traditionally been objects of curiosity. You need only attend one of these "tours" and see the obviously resentful patients to know that your curiosity has been satisfied at the expense of trespassing upon the private lives of people who desire to be left alone and not have their maladies put on display before uninvited strangers. *Eyes, official and unofficial, constantly probing and watching—such tutelage seems the fate of those who fall into that other world called asylums.*

On the other hand, these same hospital officials often react with unexpected solicitude concerning privacy when the visitor in question seeks to probe not the patient's intimacies but the institution's practices. The state of Massachusetts sought an injunction against the showing of the film *Titicut Follies,* which depicted all too graphically the miserable state of human confinement at the Bridgewater State Mental Institution on the grounds that the movie invaded the patients' privacy. This same argument was used by a California institution which fought to keep a legal service agency out of its wards until threatened with closure by a judge. Not only the right to personal modesty but the right to legal counsel is deemed by some as beyond the competence of the mentally ill. After all, they say, the mentally ill are not first of all persons but *patients.* They should be pliable and grateful.

This "therapist" perspective upon the inmate is surely the deepest part of his humiliation. To be "under eyes" all the time is already personally undermining. The inward collapse is hastened when those eyes practice a persistent paternalism, requiring that the patient-doctor game be played with proper deference. Consider the actual case of a midwestern hospital for the criminally insane. During an interview a therapist attempted at great length to compel an unwilling patient to admit his guilt to an unsolved murder. The patient stubbornly refused to discuss the case. Later, at a hospital staff conference where the patient's case was being reviewed for possible discharge, his "therapist" advised against it on the grounds that the patient's refusal to admit his guilt indicated a "lack of insight" into his pathological drives. Sometime after the request for discharge was denied, the hospital learned from the police that another person confessed and the patient in question was cleared of suspicion. His earlier refusal, contrary to indicating illness, was in fact a sign of his internal strength, his determination to hold on to reality—even against an "authority" on reality. But all this strength had been turned against him. He was too private, held his ground too stubbornly. And since he was obviously "a patient," that signaled resistance to proper therapeutic performance.

Professor Goffman, after spending several months analyzing the interpersonal system of a mental hospital, summarized his conclusions: "When the inmate loses control over who observes him in his predicament or knows about his past, he is being contaminated by a forced relationship to these people."[13] Such personal stripping, such forced intimacy destroys inner reserve. It reduces self-disclosure to a pedestrian nonchalance. The self receives itself as a superficiality, a kind of shameless performance;

in Doris Lessing's phrase, "a nothing but." Stigmatizing has done its humbling work and eroded the self's persuasion of its own seriousness and solidity. There's just no "I" left inside to celebrate, no mystery. Goffman concludes his observations with this shattering irony.

> The moral career of the mental patient has unique interest; it can illustrate the possibility that in casting off the raiments of the old self—or in having this cover torn away—the person need not seek a new role and a new audience before which to cower. Instead he can learn, at least for a time, to practice before all groups the amoral arts of shamelessness.[14]

With no face left to save, the patient is "free"; an attentive, indeed a promiscuous performer—cured by inanity.

Degradation

Perhaps, as Doctor Szasz has suggested, it's time to de-professionalize the language of mental care. "Patient," "hospital," "treatment"—all this is the talk of extraordinary dependency. And dependency, at least in our culture, is viewed as degrading, as the last resort of those who have lost all pride. Consider the situation of the welfare recipient. *Welfare is most of the time warfare.* Somebody's getting taken. Usually it's the recipient who caves in, becomes pliable, and sleeps around a lot, by way of self-commentary.

In a certain sense the giver must always turn his face away at the moment of giving. It's a way of refusing to make the other into an *object* of our generosity rather than *his own* dignified *subject.* The welfare system clearly has little sense for such niceties of self-esteem. Not only is the recipient viewed as an object of official pity; he's suspect as one who steals from the public. There's no sensitivity to what such handling steals in return—a person's face. In fact, personal reserve seems to be viewed in our society less as a right than as a privilege, a privilege conferred by the self-consciously inconspicuous upon the determinedly conventional. We have already seen how those who receive a socially distinctive label such as "mentally ill" (it could as well have been "celebrity," "criminal," or "hero") find themselves suddenly removed from otherwise taken-for-granted rights of personal privacy and distance. This same quality of being constantly *pried at* is the subtle, daily degradation imposed upon the welfare recipient.

Disclosing assets and resources, revealing the names of one's friends and associates, submitting to investigations and questioning, accounting for expenditures and social behavior—these are the prices of receiving welfare. Loss of privacy is loss of dignity, and it's part of the shame of being a welfare recipient.[15]

Unfortunately, if the federal government has its way, this shaming will soon become a good deal more efficient. A recent study sponsored by the National Academy of Science published its concern (in *Databanks in a Free Society*) about the welfare reform sought by the present administration. The new program would centralize the welfare system especially as regards eligibility and verification. By computerizing the dossiers on the estimated twenty-six million persons receiving aid and networking information from the Internal Revenue Service, Social Security Administration, Veterans Administration, Department of Labor, unemployment offices, case investigators, and so on—the administration promises to monitor the public *largess* with precision. Everyone involved will be carefully located and minutely tracked. As the Academy of Science researchers soon discovered, throughout all this enthusiasm for keeping track of people, very little thought was given to the protection of privacy: such things as record accuracy and access, length of retention and rights of challenge and expungement, the permissible forms of investigative surveillance, the boundaries of relevant information, the right to challenge termination of aid, and the degree of personal information networking compatible with a free society. As the report concludes,

We may be creating one of the largest, most sensitive, and highly computerized record systems in the nation's history, without explicit protections for the civil liberties of millions of persons whose lives will be profoundly affected.[16]

It's not just systems that get abused. Persons can, too. The situation demands a very careful balancing by administrators who prize efficiency, but even more, personal dignity.

The religious and humanitarian commitments of our culture admonish us to help the poor. We do not help a man, however, by giving him bread at the price of demanding his personal integrity. Generosity must be generous in its style of giving or else it is not humanly freeing but enslaving. The Old Testament writers sensed something of this in speaking about a God who not only forgives but *forgets*. It is that graciousness, that friendliness for life, which lets the past pass away and become truly past, and so opens the future in a way we earlier thought impossible. We would do well to greet with some suspicion, therefore, the passion of minute inquiry, the passion of unveiling, the collection of permanent personal dossiers that converts every future already into the past, that degrades at the moment of what it thinks of as its "generosity."

Welfare has become mostly warfare. The victims are mostly the defenseless, who have their defenses shorn from them as the price of their dependency. If there's a sacredness to life, an awesomeness, so to speak, in a person's dying, then too many of us are officially required to die at an early age.

Self-Esteem

Humiliation drains and impoverishes us. It has the smell of death in it. Self-esteem builds us up, vitalizes us toward life—our own and others, encourages a lively and generous ego. In *Love and Will* psychiatrist Rollo May comments ironically upon the fact that magazines like *Glamour* and *Playboy* have succeeded only in transferring the fig leaf from the human genitals to the human face. This facelessness, this fear to be as oneself, this loss in intensity of focus and transaction with life has puzzled social critics. One of them, Kenneth Keniston, thinks it has to do with a loss of nerve. What's needed, he says, is "the courage to be *for* something despite the perishability and transience of all human endeavors." And this requires "the courage to risk being wrong, to risk doing unintentional harm, and, above all, the courage to overcome one's own humility and sense of finite inadequacy."[17] This makes a nice point: *self-esteem is in part an overcoming*.

Many experience modern culture as overwhelming. Yet we are the only creatures on our planet who must *stage* our world to live it, energize its drama of shared meaning by our conviction, and fund it with our serious attention. For us, this humbling, this *loss of will to play our world,* signals, if sustained, a withdrawal of the species from itself, a de-volution. For our species arose as a kind of exuberance, a *self-enjoyment externalizing itself upon reality*. And this is the other part of basic self-esteem: an overcoming, yes; but also a sense of *bold belonging*. Put simply, self-esteem is the conviction that *we are meant this way,* that the world is *for us*—a generosity extending itself toward our self-display, a proper place to "show our face" in.

Self-loss

There are, to be sure, many who think we don't belong here this way, that this boldness represents our species' fundamental mistake, its sin. The Calvinist religious heritage speaks for this point of view, although we could as well have chosen others from both Western and Eastern religions. In a famous passage from his *Institutes* the Genevan reformer summarizes his view of man. "We are not our own," Calvin proclaims, "therefore, as far as possible, let us forget ourselves and the things that are ours. . . . Let this, then, be the first step, to abandon ourselves, and devote the whole energy of our minds to the service of God." [18] Man is here advised, insofar as he is able, to expunge all boldness of his being and replace it with a proper docility toward God. The world is not a place open to man's staging, but a place of divine ordinance to which man is to be broken and conformed.

Still, the face which cannot see *itself* reflected in its works remains profoundly veiled from its own reality. It thinks of its works as not its own even as it does them, in this case religious ones. Thus, humility can express a blinding self-inflation: the notion of being inhabited, possessed, and securely directed by an Other—by a Supremacy. You can see this is a comforting thought for a creature unable to coincide with itself and so sticking out alone among its slumbering fellow planet mates. Yet it is our species' peculiar task to survive only by *becoming aware* of our activities and so freeing ourselves from entrapment within our past productions. This ability allowed us to emerge quite suddenly out of the winnowing of an Ice Age, which crushed so many other species more securely encrusted within their instinctual encodings. We arose as a kind of freedom creature, *self*-directing.[19]

Indeed, what seems at work in all this self-inflicted humiliation is precisely a gigantic but misplaced attempt at self-control—a suspicious and parsimonious fear that our still untamed insides might burst forth in a flood tide of anarchy and shame. We should not miss the irony in this, that the supposedly anti-Puritanical Sigmund Freud nevertheless held much the same position. In his *Civilization and Its Discontents* he expressed this same idea that man has inherited a fundamentally explosive inside (an "id") which needs constant controlling if civilization is to survive. Only now the controllers are ego therapists rather than trainers in divine docility.

But this attempt at control doesn't work. For those who find nothing of joy and curiosity inside themselves are constantly driven to seek distraction, a place *outside* to place themselves. And this need leads to a fetishizing of life: seeking to lose oneself in God, or in a cause, or more popularly these days, in one's possessions. The inability to apply oneself actively to life, *to play the world,* leads to the attempt to found oneself *from outside in.* It's an astonishing discovery—that the fundamental movement of self-estimate in both *Glamour* and in Calvin are *the same:* to receive oneself as one who is sovereignly watched.

Fetishism and effectiveness

The fetishist seems at first glance one who showers a ridiculous amount of care and anxiety upon a pathetically narrow corner of meaning. He fawns over a vest or a car; he dreams of a knee. But looked at more closely, fetishism has less to do with the magnitude of significance in the object of fascination than a reversal in the order of authority—the object comes to define the subject. Karl Marx saw this happening in the overall structure of modern production: the active producer becomes the passive product of his former productions. Biblical writers spoke of this as idolatry—false devotion. And the best of them, although not all biblical writers were the best, knew that the most powerful forms of idolatry come only at the higher reaches of object significance.

Indeed the fetish of religion, the idol of the spirit, is the highest form, the most perfect transfer of the self outside of itself. Theologian Paul Tillich saw this. "Much courage to be, created by religion," he pointed out, "is nothing else than the desire to limit one's own being and to strengthen this limitation through the power of religion."[20] Such fetishism of the spirit seeks at heart to avoid the anxiety of effectiveness—namely, the possibility of mistake, of failure, and most fundamentally, the shaking perception of that finitude which swallows in forgetfulness all our best efforts. Unable to believe in his competence to fill the world with his own creative meanings, the fetishist seeks safety in surrender, in release from belonging to himself. He is afraid of life and backs off from himself so as not to have to *show his face.*

We can find a concrete example of this tendency in the recent rise of a fetishism of physical well-being. What does this explosion of health spas, weight watchers, cholesterol counters, health foods, athletics at noon, and jogging in the morning all add up to? We might conclude that it merely shows a proper self-esteem, the attempt to nurture one's vital powers and so prolong personal effectiveness. Yet looked at more closely, the opposite seems more often the case: health is sought for health's sake in a world bereft of public meanings that might win us into self-abandon and exhaustion. If we are, at heart, creatures of play, seeking a kind of free intensity, an alertness and focus, a sense of awe as we are drawn mightily into dramas laden with significance, then preoccupation with physical health represents a profound timidity. It is the loss of psychic largeness, a kind of lowest common denominator for a culture which has lost faith in public values that transcend a person's narrow well-being.

Ours is a time, it seems, when physicians and turnkeys gain enormously in authority because they preside over our bodies— shuffling ushers in a sanctuary whose god has departed. The nineteenth-century German social critic Max Stirner gave powerful voice to this insight.

> When one is anxious only to live, he easily, in this solicitude, forgets the enjoyment of life. If his only concern is for life, and he thinks "if only I have my dear life," he does not apply his full strength to using, that is, enjoying, life. But how does one use life? In using it up, like the candle, which one uses in burning it up. One uses life, and consequently himself the living one, in *consuming* it and himself. *Enjoyment of life* is using life up.[21]

Here is a sense of bold belonging, an exhilarating sense of exhausting oneself in weaving one's insides lavishly into the external world. For man to be fully alive he must practice not only a biological but also a species being—the expressive art of creatively impressing his meanings upon reality. It's the only way we have of really saying "yes" to ourselves. Compared to it, the privatized self-affirmation of popular psychology remains a kind of apology.

Reflected in the boldness of our species calling, preoccupation with physical health appears but a consolation prize for a world no longer able to offer us persuasive higher pursuits. We become absorbed in narrow projects of meaning whose ultimate reality is a crushing finitude. This turn of events demonstrates the need to rehabilitate in some meaningful form the metaphor of "eternal life"—a destiny higher than the timidity of a self-consciousness trapped within its body's fragilities. But such a rehabilitation must avoid the surrender often previously required—to wit, "I'll promise to let you live my life for me, if only I don't have to do my own dying."

In fact to do one's own living is precisely to *move consciously into our finitude:* our finitude of foresight and of charity, our finitude of power. It is to experience fully not just our authority, but also our ineluctable limits. One of the seductions of timidity of life, of psychic parsimoniousness, is the avoidance of having to struggle at these barriers, while living boldly necessarily implies experiencing directly one's personal and historical limits. One of these boundaries we should look at here, because it bears directly upon the question of self-esteem in the context of the active life, is moral failure. To live a vigorous life of unfolding oneself into the world is to live in vital interaction with others. Personal effectiveness is not a Promethean anarchy of energy or a vision of splendor that cannot communicate itself. *Effectiveness is the persuasive inviting of others to participate in the joint staging of new and richer meanings.* Thus, it is life beyond safety, life which must learn to affirm itself even in the midst of the pain of hurting and being hurt.

Such affirmation comes both from within and from beyond the interpersonal situation. It is the self's reaffirming its reliance upon itself even after defeat, daring again, so to speak, to take hold and steer its life. At the same moment, it is higher *intimacy* with those life processes which transcend every immediacy and draw us into the tranquillity of a more distanced perspective. J. Glenn Gray in his book *The Warriors* senses the healing offered to moral failure by these moments of intimacy with more ultimate horizons. Commenting upon the awesome moral burdens of the combat soldier, Gray concludes:

> watching the stars at night, as soldiers often have to do on lonely guard duty or in their foxholes, can rob one of the arrogance that makes men believe their history is the beginning and end of the things that are. . . . Far from making a man sad and defeatist, this perspective can instil a kind of serenity. . . . the confidence that, even if we vanish from the earth sooner or later as a consequence of our failures, that, too, will be within the compass of a Being incomparably greater and more enduring than the race of man.[22]

Unlike the fetishist, who seeks security by fastening upon an external object of devotion, those who know something of belonging to themselves can let themselves go to a future that, in order to be future, remains *its own* and not ours.

Intimacy and self-reliance

Intimacy with broader horizons of meaning can help heal moral failure, but it presupposes *intimacy between persons*. For it is in interpersonal encounter that we first learn to take joy in, and thus to energize this "I" that unfolds the distances of inner space necessary for self-judgment. It is a witness to the fact that before we can accuse ourselves we must first have learned, however brokenly, to affirm ourselves. *The opposite of guilt is not self-love but indifference, slight self-attentiveness.* Interpersonal sharing is one of those "areas" which positively encourages our self-esteem and internal vitality. It is where we learn to take seriously "who we are."

Such intimacy implies a necessary privacy, an exclusivity. It is the opposite of that exhibitionism which seeks to get itself off its hands by a kind of leap into exposure. Intimacy is cautious, preserving the distance between selves instead of collapsing it, precisely because it has learned the enrichment of *sharing secrets*. The self which seeks to give itself away, or get the other to, has nothing to give or receive thereafter. Intimacy is a sustained reciprocity of each providing entrance to the other, and so implies a certain equality in power of being. Each must "grow" into the other person's strengths. Each must refuse to shame the other's strengths as "a betrayal" and refuse in turn to be shamed by those strengths as "incompetent." Thus, interpersonal sharing implies a polarity, a dialectic between self-reliance and dependence upon another.

That true intimacy wins our willing dependence upon another no one who has experienced it can deny. Our inner space becomes a more generous and friendly place to us, so that we come to rely upon the other as a way of liking ourselves. Yet it is also true that there is simply more of us than can exhaust itself in any single relationship. At the heart of even the most perfect intimacy lies this unbridgeable solitude—the more known and felt because of intimacy's intense attention. Our inner space, even as we depend fundamentally upon the other, is also thrown back upon itself. Union, the attempt to merge two selves in an "engulfing we" is not the fulfillment of love but the collapse of the internal distances that feed mature caring. For *the self must belong to and rely upon itself in order to give of itself without giving itself away.*

Self-reliance is an old companion in the library of the American mind. Ralph Waldo Emerson, who has been called "the first philosopher of the American spirit," named one of his most famous essays after the idea. "You take the way from man, not to man," he argued.[23] Each must come at last to know himself as his own center. Emerson pointed out: "There is time in every man's education when he arrives at the conviction that envy is ignorance; that imitation is suicide; that he must take himself for better, for worse, as his portion." [24] It is an education in learning to belong to oneself, to rely upon oneself—not as some perfection of wisdom or virtue, which no man is—but as in any case one's inevitable base. No amount of external praise, no collection of experiences, no museum of world travels can bring this sense of inner fullness and self-regard. Each of us is our own journey. "Travelling is a fool's paradise," Emerson said. "Our first journeys discover to us the indifference of places. . . . My giant goes with me wherever I go." [25]

Self-reliance is at bottom an awe that absorbs both shame and praise into that strange equanimity of self-reflection—that witnessing of our lives through remembered years, events, and faces which can never be held and pondered in just this way again—a sense of precious finitude. It is the lesson not only of what we have done but also of what we have sustained and survived. Blows to our self-esteem, we discover, can provide curious reverse impetus for the self's discovery that it can, despite it all, still rely upon itself—and must. Momentarily we can be overwhelmed. Who has not? But in retrospect the lesson turns opposite: that we can survive being overwhelmed. We discover ourselves as the mystery of our own remembrance, this solitary witness whose story is unprecedented and wholly incapable of full recounting. In this sense, Emerson saw, we are our own instructors. "We must go alone. I like the silent church before the service begins better than any preaching." [26]

We can justly criticize Emerson for an excessive individualism. But it remains true: when a man dies, a whole continent sinks. No communalism can hide this fact, nor for long successfully make up for the loss. Intimacy and self-reliance are not contradictions but necessary companions.

Consciousness, commitment, and power—these are the tools, if Professor Etzioni is correct, of the active life and society.[27] Of consciousness, we have just spoken at length. Of that commitment which the self confers upon the task of its own voyage, we have begun to reflect and will return to later. Now we must take up the third item, *power*, and that shared commitment to common purposes which births its public attainment. Self-esteem must display itself by externalizing itself into the world. Without this "politics," it maintains itself only through a kind of martyrdom, almost as a resident alien. Either of these represents a crippling price, a self inordinately dwelling upon itself without public expression and expansion, without ventilation of satiated self-preoccupation.

4

Private Association and Human Freedom

Under modern political conditions the citizens have only a restricted
share in the public business of the state, yet it is essential to provide
men . . . with business of a public character over and above their
private business. This work, which the modern state does not always
provide, is found in private association.
—Friedrich Hegel, *Philosophy of Right*

If someone asked us to recount our country's "public riches," we
would likely be puzzled and silent at first. Then we might mention
something about gold at Fort Knox. But mostly we would remain
uncomfortable with the idea. We are not as aware of the treasury of
public benefits as were the people of classical Greece. An old Greek
adage says something to the effect that "a man alone is an idiot."
This saying reflects their persuasion that man's humanness is
constituted in the fact that he is a public being. Jean-Jacques
Rousseau spoke for this tradition in *The Social Contract:* "The
passing from the state of nature to the civil state produces in man a
very remarkable change, by substituting justice for instinct in his
conduct, and giving to his actions a moral character which they
had lacked before."[1]

To the classical mind, it is by way of his essential "publicness"
that man first becomes rational and free. Citizenship, participation
in public discourse, is what de-privatizes man's existence and so
enlarges and ennobles him. The English conservative, Edmund
Burke, who looked with less than full enthusiasm upon the
volcanic rise of modern individualism, spoke eloquently on this.
Society should be looked upon "with reverence," he said, because

75

society is not just a transitory partnership for purposes of expediency. Rather, society is based upon partnership in all aspects of life and culture. Burke contended that not only was this a partnership that was vital among those living as contemporaries, but also that the partnership extended across the years from those who had lived before and were dead to those who were yet to be born.[2] In seeking to defend man's autonomy, the dignity of his inner space, we must not confuse privacy with solipsism, the internal slumbering of mere "naturalness" with vigorous human selfhood.

Community and Freedom

The lessons of loyalty, holding on to our deeds and comrades while also guarding our personal integrity, the lessons of accountability, of long-range solidarity with colleagues whose judgment we esteem and from whom we gain some objectivity concerning ourselves, lessons of mutual encouragement as well as mutual correction, and those sometimes heavy moments of parting when we must say "No, there I cannot follow you"—all these rich humanizing experiences are the fruit of our private *associational life.* Here we gain freedom from the moral ineptitude of idiosyncrasy, the arbitrariness of undiscussed certainties. Michael Walzer of Harvard senses well these human benefits of community. He speaks of it as

> the art of overcoming pride and every sort of individual caprice while still associating honorable men—comrades who fulfill their commitments whenever they can, who take their commitments very seriously, but who have reasons for committing themselves, which they also take seriously. . . . The solidarity of such men is fragile, for it depends not only on the principles they share, the promises they have made, and the respect they have for one another, but also on the respect they have for themselves, for their own intelligence and judgment.[3]

It is precisely this kind of honorable associational life that many view as the seedbed of democracy. On the one side, such associations protect the self from naked exposure to and dependency upon the overall social system and its sometimes wise but ofttimes foolish myths of public meaning. Meaningful community life breaks open and pluralizes the social landscape. It is an instrument of transcendence. On the other side, the disciplines of associational life educate the individual to public responsibility, moving him beyond narrow self-preoccupations into broader experiences of satisfaction and competence. Vital communities provide then both *training* in the arts of public life and *shelter* from totalized dependency. They break up any monopoly of socialization. As such, voluntary associations are what make and keep citizen consent a political force and reality. And without consent of an informed citizenry there is no democracy.

Now we must suffer from a certain determined myopia not to see how threatened in this respect our heritage of freedom has presently become. The late C. Wright Mills saw it starting.

> The executive ascendancy in economic, military, and political institutions has lowered the effective use of all those voluntary associations which operate between the state and the economy on the one hand, and the family and the individual in the primary group on the other.[4]

This executive ascendancy—what we have called elsewhere in this book "the administrative state"—tends to reduce our associational life to a kind of lonely crowd. We become undefended consumers of the overall social system. Rehabilitation of community, revival of "conviviality" (see below), must be high on the agenda of anyone who prizes freedom more than efficiency and the development of human virtue more than the swift delivery of shallow satisfactions.

But more than executive ambition these days invades and corrupts the vitality of our associational lives. A suspicious paternalism is characteristic of some of our political leaders—a passion to unveil the interior conversations of opposing groups while holding tightly to their own secrecy.

One of the difficulties we have in defending ourselves here is that our law, informed as it is by the public philosophy of liberal individualism, has difficulty focusing on the protection of associational privacy as something distinct from privacy of the individual and his property. A recent article in the *Yale Law Journal* makes this clear. The author points out that while the Court has sought to protect the right of individuals to free speech as integral to the process of democracy, it has "taken for granted the freedom from potential inhibition of [a] second stage—*the listener's decision-making in light of received information....*" As the author says, "The Court's assumption seems to be that speech need only reach the listener's ear for the free expression system of democracy to operate successfully."[5]

But this ignores the fact that we usually don't "listen" alone. We consider, weigh, decide, and otherwise go about the tasks of self-government *in association with our trusted colleagues.* Justice Douglas has recognized the need here for developing a wider legal imagination and extending the protection of privacy to man's associational life as well. "Two principles," he argued in his dissent in *United States* v. *Caldwell,* "are at stake here. One is that the people, the ultimate governors, must have absolute freedom of, and therefore privacy of, their individual opinions and beliefs. . . ." But then he adds:

> Ancillary to that principle is the conclusion that an individual must also have absolute privacy over whatever information he may generate in the course of testing his opinions and beliefs . . . [for] effective self-government cannot succeed unless the people are immersed in a steady, robust, unimpeded, and uncensored flow of opinion and reporting which are continuously subjected to critique, rebuttal, and reexamination.[6]

Unfortunately, Justice Douglas remains thus far in the minority of the Court on this point.

Invasions of Associational Privacy

That privacy of association is at present insufficiently protected either by law or common practice can be illustrated in three concrete ways: (1) the investigatory grand jury, (2) the use of government informers, and (3) political espionage and intimidation.

Trial by grand jury

> I want you to describe for the jury every occasion during the year 1970 when you have been in contact with, attended meetings that were conducted by, or been any place where any individual spoke whom you knew to be associated with or affiliated with the Students for a Democratic Society, the Weatherman, the Communist party, or any other organization advocating the overthrow of the United States, describing for the grand jury when the incidents occurred, who was present, and what was said by all members present there, and what you did at the times you were in those meetings, groups, associations or conversations.[7]

This is an actual question put to a young radical by the federal prosecutor before an investigative grand jury in Ann Arbor. As we shall see, compelling a person to unveil his associational life with this unspecific, "fishing expedition" type inquiry is a potent weapon not simply of general government surveillance but of government attack upon dissenting communities. What a long way this is from where the grand jury began.

Thomas Jefferson and James Madison insisted on including grand juries in the Fifth Amendment to the Bill of Rights in order to provide a "people's panel" to protect potential defendants against ambitious or corrupt prosecutors and unwarranted prosecutions. In fact, however, the grand jury in its investigatory role first became of wide use in the 1920s as an instrument to break up the organization of labor. From this rather unsavory adolescence, its reputation improved in the mid-sixties as part of a universally accepted government attack on organized crime. Through the awesome power of subpoena and immunity, the grand jury proved an effective weapon in undoing that comradeship of silence which preserved the conspiracy that organizes crime.

All this seemed fair enough at the time. After all, the associated members of a conspiracy had banded together out of the pursuit of individual interest. Bringing legal pressure to bear in such a fashion as to tip the scale of interest away from silence and so expose the conspiracy to law enforcement proceedings seemed simply to shift the stakes in the game of self-interest already agreed upon by the associated members. But what happens when this prosecutory arsenal is turned upon a community whose primary bond is a shared philosophy or common politics?

We find an example of this in the Harrisburg grand-jury investigation of the Berrigan case. Sister Jogues Egan was asked a series of wide-ranging, unspecific questions about her fellow nun, Elizabeth McAlister. She refused to testify, saying she could not and would not betray the confidence of her friendship. She was put in jail and, except for release on a technicality, would have had to remain there for the eighteen-month life of the grand jury. Here the subpoena and immunity power was brought to bear upon a comradeship of value allegiance, not an alliance of self-interests. The grand jury changed the game of calculating individual advantage into a very different game. It got itself into the business of coercing conscience, undermining individual integrity by inducing betrayal of friends, attacking community.

Perhaps the effect is unintended, but the consequence of this use of the grand jury can be very "political" indeed. Precisely such associations of moral seriousness and public action are the backbone of social pluralism. They break open the monopoly of public opinion and so provide "room" for the possibility of true citizen consent. Government "by consent of the governed" implies a multiplicity of public perspectives on critical political issues, a multiplicity of groups actively pushing their point of view, organizing others to their persuasion, and seeking effective public presentation. Professor Walzer sees the danger in using the grand jury to subvert such groups. "It undermines the moral basis of pluralism," he points out, "if the members perform as demanded, violating their consciences and selling out their fellow-members. For pluralism requires the integrity of conscience."[8]

But isn't the real issue criminal activity? The grand jury is simply investigating possible *crime*. And crime is *not* part of the legitimate activity of political dissent.

This is true, but only in part. Prosecutors can use grand juries to go on fishing expeditions, as in the Ann Arbor case, without specified focus on a specific or suspected crime. A. William Olson, recent head of the Internal Security Division of the Justice Department said as much. "In many cases," he said,

> you go into an investigative grand jury with only a suspicion that criminal laws have been violated. And sometimes as the grand jury progresses you get bits and pieces. And sometimes they fit in not with what you started out to investigate, but with other crimes, not necessarily in the same jurisdiction.[9]

But what if the process doesn't lead to indictments, or only very shaky ones later denied by jury? How do you draw the line between investigating possible violation of law and conducting general political surveillance and intelligence gathering? Leslie Bacon, we were told, was thought to know something about the bombing of the Capital in Washington. But once before the grand jury, she was asked mostly about her acquaintances and wide associations with the New Left.

Moreover, this bringing of a cloud of investigation and forced testimony down around the communities of radical war protest and advocates of New Left politics has proved politically shattering to them. As students earlier became hesitant to attend protest rallies, fearing to be photographed and dossiered, now they feared befriending known radicals. They became hesitant about discussing options for political action, of joining groups of serious dissent. The effect of such grand jury investigations—whatever their intentions—was to cut the dissenting communities off from their recruiting base, to *privatize alienation*, depriving it of group focus and support. It encouraged a kind of public silence. The danger that lies in this direction was well stated by Albert Camus. "Only the word fed by blood and heart can unite men, whereas the silence of tyrannies separates them. Tyrants indulge in monologues over millions of solitudes."[10]

Clearly, this whole grand-jury area needs careful thought by administrators of justice who seek also that the justice they administer preserves and nourishes democracy. They will want to avoid any eroding of freedom's foundation in the vital pluralism of opinion and the associational life that sustains and empowers it. Privacy of association, the integrity of conscience of the associated members, the seclusion of conversations between comrades which sometimes confirm but ofttimes correct the foolish enthusiasms of individual members—all this is of profound human and social benefit. Unfortunately, there is evidence that some recent grand-jury use has done violence to these values, and not simply inadvertently but perhaps with malice of forethought, i.e., to suppress political activity. Witness:

> Tell the grand jury every place you went after you returned to your apartment from Cuba, every city you visited, with whom and by what means of transportation, and whom you visited during the time of your travels after you left your apartment in Ann Arbor, Mich., in May of 1970.[11]

We are faced here with an issue of prosecutory discretion and of professional legal ethics which can bring internal discipline to bear against the political misuse of the instruments of law. Surely greater attention must be given to grand jury "fishing expeditions" that are only vaguely related to suspected criminal activity, especially when moving in politically sensitive areas. Relevance and specificity of testimony are criteria which help differentiate the political misuse of grand juries from the appropriate investigation of possible politically connected crimes, as in the case of former Vice-President Agnew. Judges can help in this regard by taking a more active, watchdog role. The right to take one's lawyer into the grand-jury room (now denied) can also help bring more discipline and focus upon the questioning. Generally, however, what we need is greater public recognition of the positive social value of associational privacy, a value that needs careful weighing alongside that other obvious social value which is effective law enforcement.

These dangers to associational life are even more vividly illustrated in the case of paid government informers who use the lifeblood of community—loyalty and trust— to unveil, attack, and destroy community.

Informer and agent provocateur

Government use of informers to keep whole areas and populations of our society under general and sustained surveillance has become a routine practice. That is an extraordinary thing to say. But just that is what is shown by documents taken from the Media, Pennsylvania, office of the FBI and subsequently published in *Win* magazine in 1972. Consider the following memo from the agent in charge of the Philadelphia office to "all Headquarters agents."

> It is essential that this office develop a large number of additional racial informants . . . sources which should be kept in mind are employees and owners of businesses in ghetto areas which might include taverns, liquor stores . . . janitors of apartment buildings, etc. The Bureau also suggests contacts with persons who frequent ghetto areas on a regular basis such as taxi drivers, salesmen and distributors of newspapers, food and beverages. Installment collectors might also be considered in this regard.[12]

We have here the open attempt to honeycomb a community, turning a "neighborhood" upside down by using its infrastructure of human services against itself, against its "neighborliness." And all this for the vague purpose of "racial informing" unrelated to any specific or suspected crime.

Moreover, from Bureau memos cited earlier we know that this same tactic has been used not just upon such otherwise expected targets as organized crime or the supply systems of lethal drugs, but also upon colleges, peace organizations, civil rights groups, and even the American Civil Liberties Union. More alarming still is the considerable evidence that the use of informers (and wiretaps and electronic bugging) is practiced *more intensively by local police agencies,* such as civil-disobedience and intelligence squads, where authorization, accountability, and record maintenance are less stringently regulated than at the federal level. It is immensely more convenient, for example, for an FBI agent to ask a favor of a local police operative than go through the elaborate procedure of securing Bureau approval to install a telephone tap or mail cover.

Part of the problem in all this is the fact that the whole question of the use of informers by police and government agencies has been left largely without Supreme Court attention. Although the Fourth Amendment to the Bill of Rights declares that persons have the right "to be secure in their persons, houses, papers and effects against unreasonable searches and seizures," it was only in 1967 that the Supreme Court concluded that this right protects a citizen's privacy in his *personal affairs (Katz* v. *U.S.).* Up to that time law-enforcement officials had been operating under the 1928 *Olmstead* decision which concluded that the Fourth Amendment protected only material things, not conversations. And even with *Katz* only "unreasonable" searches and seizures are prohibited.

With the passage of the Omnibus Crime Control and Safe Streets Act of 1968 the regulations on eavesdropping and wiretapping have been significantly strengthened. But in a decision in 1971 *(U.S.* v. *White)* the Supreme Court refused to extend this kind of stringent regulation to the case of informers. The Court reasoned that the suspect did not intend to keep secret conversations made to a known person, from that person, and therefore the suspect "bore the risk" that his supposed friend might be an informer. The irony of this decision may be the dwindling of wiretapping and electronic eavesdropping only to be replaced by an explosive expansion of relatively unsupervised networks of informers.

We know, for example (again from the Media FBI files), that a local FBI agent is free to initiate and maintain informers without authorization of a superior if payment does not exceed $300 per month. When we stop to think just how much $300 a month represents to a poor person or to a college student, or mail clerk or telephone switchboard operator, we should begin to question the public need for such unsupervised and unspecific general monitoring. Three hundred dollars represents an immensely attractive inducement to enter into the system of informing, of turning the private worlds of one's unsuspecting associates into the raw material of public sleuthing. And this is to say nothing of the demonstrated function of such monetary inducement upon the transformation of an informer into an *agent provocateur* in order to keep agency benefits flowing in.

There have been three recent and celebrated cases, all involving the antiwar movement, which came to depend essentially upon a government informer who in the process of informing became a *provocateur.* These are the Berrigan case, in which a group of priests and nuns were accused of plotting to kidnap Henry Kissinger; the draft-board conspiracy case of the Camden 28; and the Florida indictment and subsequent trial of the Vietnam Veterans Against the War, for plotting disruption of the 1972 Republican Convention. Significantly, all three cases, when submitted to the test of trial and defense cross-examination, failed of conviction. In each, the jury either refused to believe the informer or found him to be the *principle mover* of the alleged illegal act, the government's creator of the government's case.

The Camden 28 trial is less widely known than the others but is more instructive of the danger because the informer, Robert Hardy, decided to testify openly for the defense.[13] Also key was the judge's unprecedented decision in his instructions to the jury to allow for a defense of "excessive government participation." Up to then, the only legal defense against an *agent provocateur* was "entrapment" with its difficult task of proving "prior innocence of mind." With the Camden case, it became enough if the jury were persuaded that alleged illegal activity would not and could not have developed without "overreaching" government participation. Not innocence of mind but *government enabling activity* became the issue. Clearly if this precedent holds up, a significant restraint will have been imposed upon the practice of informers, at least upon their usefulness in gaining conviction by creating the case involving the crime with which their unsuspecting comrades are charged.

In the Camden case, the informer testified that he first associated himself with the group when they had become thoroughly discouraged about ever entering the Camden draft board to destroy draft files. He told the jury that without his constant encouragement, his drawing of detailed and ingenious plans for the break-in (some of which he got from the FBI), and his supplying of tools, food, and transportation (all reimbursed by the FBI), the raid would never have taken place. Moreover, informer Hardy revealed a macabre world of higher politics moving in the shadows behind the scenes of local agency officials. Hardy had been promised, so he testified, that his friends would be arrested on a practice run (on August 14) before the actual break-in (a week later) and subsequently charged only with "conspiracy." In this way, he could think of himself as actually protecting what he viewed as his morally compassionate but foolish companions. Indeed, under oath, the Camden FBI office admitted to having eighty agents in and around the building where the draft board was located on August 14. But no arrests were made. At the last minute the agents were instructed by higher-ups to wait until the actual raid took place. As a local agent reported to a furious Hardy, "someone at the little White House in California" *wanted the raid to happen.*

After hearing the case, the jury acquitted all defendants on all charges. And that was before they and we had access to the Watergate testimony of former White House chief of staff, H. R. (Bob) Haldeman. In it he indicated a curious affection for possible violent protest ("good") directed at the president, and obscene language ("great") hurled at Billy Graham—words he penned in the margin of a briefing memo sent by an advance man preparing for a Nixon visit to a Graham rally in Charlotte, North Carolina.

After Watergate the political use of law to stifle domestic dissent can no longer be viewed as the peculiar occupational paranoia of radical political types. Dr. Ellsberg's psychiatrist's office was burglarized—on instructions from the White House. The infamous Huston domestic intelligence plan did receive presidential OK. Special Internal Revenue Service audits were made upon listed "enemies" at White House request. Daniel Schorr of CBS television news was subjected to full FBI investigation because of what was considered his antiadministration point of view. At the Berrigan trial, at the Camden 28 trial, and at the Florida trial of the Vietnam Veterans Against the War we have seen what an undisciplined administration can do with the legally ill-defined and so undisciplined territory of informers. There is ample evidence that the time is ripe to correct such abuses by congressional and Court action.

The task does not seem too difficult. Informers are an important tool in the effective maintenance of law. And they are a legitimate tool when properly authorized, supervised, and restrained in their activity. Rules for doing this should begin by recognizing that there are several types or classes of informers:

1. the private citizen who is an accidental witness to criminal activity and reports this activity to the police

2. the private citizen who is an accidental witness to activity of interest to law enforcement agencies and upon questioning reveals such activity

3. the private citizen who without solicitation on the part of law enforcement agencies is an intentional witness to activity of interest to law enforcement agencies and who for various reasons reveals this activity, but without maintaining surveillance further

4. the individual (private citizen or law enforcement agent) who establishes and/or maintains a relationship for the express purpose of being a witness to activities of others and who reveals such activity to law enforcement agencies, with or without personal benefit, on a sustained basis

The first two categories do not need and, given their contingent character, probably could not effectively receive regulation. The latter two types are more difficult. There is an element of trust established between the informer and those he informs upon in both these types of surveillance. In example number three, the trust is breached on the individual's own initiative and the relationship severed at that point. There is no solicitation on the part of law-enforcement agencies and no ongoing betrayal of confidence on the part of the informer. This kind of "risk" seems integral to the nature of associational life; and here the established rubric of the Supreme Court that "the suspect bears the risk" seems appropriate.

However, as regards the fourth category, new and more stringent regulation seems clearly to be called for. Here the trust relationship is either fraudulent from the beginning or becomes so and is maintained as such under official sanction and instruction. There is clearly an interjection into an intended private relationship the presence of a third entity without the permission or knowledge of the observed. In terms of the transformation of human confidences into their opposite, with the consequent radical undermining of the integrity of personal and group relationships, this type of police and government activity is of more critical social and moral import than wiretap or electronic bugging. This is because it attacks the human roots of vital associational life—trust and openness between persons. When we suspect one another, community life begins to shrivel. We start to double-think; we grow silent. And in silence lies moral arbitrariness and unchecked individual caprice.

In such cases, therefore, the invasion of privacy by informer should be sanctioned only upon proof of "probable cause" and upon approval by a judge and continuing supervision by a court. Indeed, the "probable cause" must here be weighed against the very serious undermining effect upon associational privacy which is engendered by this type of informer and the public effect such suspicions (whatever the realities) have upon the climate of democratic freedom. Especially is this the case in politically sensitive areas where under no circumstances should an informer be approved by a court for some ill-defined or general monitoring, but only on grounds of the most concrete evidence relating to criminal or potential criminal activity.

This presupposes, of course, a desire on the part of officials to maintain the power of democracy beyond simply maximizing their own power. Political espionage and intimidation, which we turn to next, is an open trespass of this democratic process. On a minor scale such activity is to be expected. But, if sustained and extensive enough, it reduces politics to administration, replacing the process of active political contention by violated and defeated integrities, by domestic passivity.

Political spying

We think immediately of Watergate. It may well be that we have seen only the tip of the iceberg. The illustration I will use here, however, has been fully revealed and was very nearly ruinous of the political life of our fourth largest city. Philadelphia began as the birthplace of our country's experiment in democratic rule and has now become, ironically, an advanced example of the attempt at one-man rule founded upon political espionage and intimidation.

Mayor Frank Rizzo, a former police commissioner, was elected to office in 1971 at the height of the "law and order" boom. He was against crime, he said. But even more, people knew, he was against student demonstrators, radicals, flower people, "uppity" blacks— anyone who lived a dream different from standard middle-class aspirations, anxieties, and mores. He seemed "tough" in times which many voters thought required tough handling. In 1971 the cause of civil liberties had few friends. Its traditional friends on the left had come to view it as the special privilege of those who can afford clever lawyers.

Two weeks after Rizzo was elected, he established, without public notice, a special thirty-three-man police squad composed of three staff inspectors, four lieutenants, twenty-two detectives, two policemen, and two policewomen. It cost a conservative estimate of $500,000 a year to operate.[14] When the whole thing came out, the mayor explained that this was a special unit "probing political corruption" and "misuse of federal funds." But the *Philadelphia Bulletin,* hardly a left-wing paper, concluded that, however it began, the special unit had in fact "evolved into a political espionage unit for Mayor Rizzo." Compared to the modest dimensions of the White House "plumbers," this was indeed big-time big brother.

If we are to believe the reports, espionage and intimidation were nothing new to Frank Rizzo. While police commissioner he was accused by his fellow Democrats and former mayors Richardson Dilworth and James Tate of bugging their telephones. At one point Rizzo is reported to have stalked into a school board meeting, demanding a policy change, and throwing a handful of files on the table, saying, "I have enough in there to ruin all of you." He has continued this practice, it seems, as mayor. At least that is what City Council President George X. Schwartz (a Democrat) and Peter J. Camiel, Democratic city chairman, have claimed. Their own personal acquaintance with the thirty-three-man police sur- veillance unit began in March of 1973. They had opposed the mayor on his selection of a candidate for district attorney— sometimes known in the language of machine politics as "the protector."

Rizzo was seeking to consolidate his hold on the party in Philadelphia. Nonetheless, what happened next, according to Rizzo, had nothing to do with his own ambitions but with other people's happily timed vices. His police squad began an intensive espionage campaign against Schwartz and Camiel which in- cluded, according to special press investigators:

—policewomen tailing female acquaintances of Schwartz in order to involve him, so Schwartz claims, "in morals scandals"

—police surveillance and listing of automobile tags of Schwartz's friends at a local country club

—the charge by Camiel and Schwartz that their telephones have been bugged (other members of City Council have said privately they suspect the same is done to them)

—extensive police interviewing of Camiel's associates and competitors in the beer business

—and the charge by Camiel and Schwartz that their offices and homes have been surreptitiously entered and searched, and that members of their family have been followed and their friends subjected to police interview.

All of this, the mayor has maintained, is either a figment of an imagination distempered by its own guilty conscience, or necessary investigation of political corruption. The latter charge has been countered by Camiel with a reverse claim of attempted political bribery by Rizzo. This charge led to one of the more amusing episodes in the whole affair. Camiel claimed that at the time of the district-attorney election Rizzo offered to let him name the architects for various upcoming city construction projects in return for his support on the mayor's choice. "Lies, lies," responded Mr. Rizzo. Offered a joint lie-detector test by a large city newspaper, the mayor cheerfully accepted saying, "I have great confidence in the polygraph. If this machine says a man lied, he lied." After the test Mr. Rizzo abruptly changed his mind about the value of such tests. It indicated that on six out of ten questions the mayor had lied, while Camiel had lied not at all.

Now as unhappy as such revelations of intensive political espionage and intimidation are, the nebulous hold on virtue characterizing many of our public servants that allows this kind of arm twisting so often to be effective is worse. It is the tactic of equally cynical partners in the same cynical game of gaining and exploiting public power. Political-scientist John Scharr analyzes why these types like to make public targets of protestors and dissenters. "Surely a large part of the zealous repression of radical protest in America," he says,

> has its roots in the fact that millions of men who are apparently "insiders" know how vulnerable the system is because they know how ambiguous their own attachments to it are. The slightest moral challenge exposes the fragile foundations of legitimacy in the modern state.[15]

Without challenge posed by strong associations of moral and political opposition, the "open spaces" of our society for citizen consent would be paved over with sophisticated power brokering. That is why it is inappropriate for us to greet all this with a responding cynicism of our own—"just politics as usual." On the scale illustrated by Mayor Rizzo it becomes *very unusual politics* indeed. It's like saying that "Watergate just shows what all politicians do." That kind of premature sophistication can land us all in chains.

This attack upon political and quasi-political association is subject to relatively simple correction. The problems can be effectively addressed by new legislative and judicial initiatives— which is not to say that such initiatives are simple to secure. But far more complex is the enervation of meaningful associational life caused by the withdrawal of effective power into more centralized systems of public transaction. Neighborhoods are under attack these days not so much consciously as unconsciously. Less and less of ourselves, so to speak, in fact resides "in our neighborhood." We are more and more dependent in our everyday lives upon centrally administered systems of production and service. If robust personal interaction in significant private association is to be rehabilitated, what is required is a quite conscious attempt to revive *conviviality* as the basic milieu of our everyday existence. This does not mean a dismantling of the industrial-bureaucratic system that characterizes all advanced industrial nations. It does mean, however, the conscious replacement of efficiency as the predominant value of these societies.

Conviviality

We depend upon the conviviality of neighborhoods, over against the abstract and often brutalizing quality of modern productive systems, to soften and humanize our touch for life. In a real sense, such informal associations are where we heal ourselves. But neighborhoods are being crushed these days under the logic of society-wide planning and efficiency. The triple ingredients of the efficient society are specialization, repetition, and hierarchy. Together, they make way for a tight structure of systematic management. But carried past a certain point, each of these trespasses basic human needs: the need for a personal sense of accomplishment, for independence and spontaneity, and for the experience of convivial community.

When former Soviet Premier Nikita Khrushchev bragged "we'll bury you all," he meant bury us in an avalanche of Soviet industrial output. What he did not notice was that the modern industrial process is beginning to *bury all of us*. That Khrushchev should make such a claim is ironic because it was Karl Marx who displayed such a firm grasp on man's need for a sense of personal accomplishment in his productive work. Marx called man "a tool-making animal." Man, he saw, is unique by the fact that he places between himself and his external environment *tools,* instruments of his active re-creation of his circumstances. Man doesn't just passively adapt. Rather, he actively changes nature to fit his own needs and fancies. He *adapts his environment;* he does not adapt to it. History begins, Marx saw, with man's production of specifically human needs, not just replicating natural ones. Man is a creature of a peculiar conviviality. For human needs can only be satisfied humanly. Accomplishment, creative initiative, and a sense of beneficent interdependence are needs fundamental to our species.

But the toolmaker is in danger of becoming a tool of his tools, a danger Marx understood all right, but mislocated in terms of twentieth-century industrial realities. Whether the means of production are owned by the individual entrepreneur or by the state, each is now "successful" according to the *same underlying logic*—the logic of efficiency, control, and prediction. Marxism and capitalism were both twins of the latter half of the nineteenth century. They share the same world of social reality. But with advanced industrialization the underlying logic of society shifts, dragging the diverse structures of ownership behind it. That is why the Soviet Union is so eager to buy our computers. In East and West, we have become fundamentally dependent upon the efficiency of our advanced "planning systems."[16] Max Weber saw this coming and diagnosed it as precisely as anyone.

> The increasing possession of goods used for consumption, and . . . an increasingly sophisticated technique of fashioning external life . . . reacts upon the standard of living and makes for an increasing subjective indispensability of organized, collective, inter-local, and thus bureaucratic, provision for the most varied wants, which previously were either unknown, or were satisfied locally or by a private economy.[17]

This elevation of our dependency into general systems of human provision leads to a depreciation of our everyday life competency. "As the power of machines increases," social-critic Ivan Illich argues, "the role of persons more and more decreases to that of mere consumers."[18] Illich calls this "radical monopoly." It happens wherever, "one industrial production process exercises an exclusive control over the satisfaction of a pressing need, and excludes nonindustrial activities from competition."[19]

We find an example of this in cars. The modern automobile has come to dominate the modes of human transportation. It has remade the shape of the city into its own image. Cars have created immense distances—distances between places of work and family places, distances between friends, distances between where we buy and where we consume what we buy. Cars make for remoteness. Their monopolizing of public space destroys the environment of feet and bicycles. Cars lead to an obsession with speed which, ironically, does not reduce but increases the amount of time each day we spend not *doing*, but getting to and from the places where we "do." As Illich concludes, "The establishment of radical monopoly happens when people give up their native ability to do what they can do for themselves and for each other . . . [It is] man's 'trivialization' by his manufactured milieu." [20]

This replacement of the milieu of conviviality—of significant interaction between persons—by a machine-consumer dependency, reflects itself at the level of our everyday language. "Housing" becomes a commodity, something we purchase rather than something we do. People *get* an education rather than learn. They *have* not only a job or fun, but sex. If a person is middle class and living in America, he can even *acquire* sensitivity. This machine-consumer interchange dominates our self-image. We are reduced to the status of system-dependent consumers, purchasing standard packages of "affluence," "education," "health," and so on.

All this represents a trespass of man's basic need for a sense of personal accomplishment and competency, for innovative re-creation of his environment, for convivial interdependency. As Illich puts it, "People need not only obtain things, they need above all the freedom to make things among which they can live, to give shape to them according to their own tastes, and to put them to use in caring for and about others." [21] "Progress" has everywhere come to mean optimizing the output of large-scale tools for people increasingly enmeshed in compulsive dependency. Tools grow powerful while persons become impotent.

The corrective to this is to re-tool our tools to fit a humanly satisfying milieu. It does not mean the end of social planning. But it does mean that planning must become a *political subject* rather than the object of expert management (see chapter 6). We must accept the criteria of human growth and personal effectiveness rather than society-wide efficiency as the key indicator of social progress. We do not have to dismantle machines, but we must discipline their use to the dimensions of the self's experience of basic competency. Sociologist Richard Sennett has seen this. We must design neighborhoods that "fit" human levels of effectiveness. Only then can a man, "use himself as a human being, make himself heard, rather than be muffled by those who are different and more skilled in the arts of bureaucratic management." [22] Decentralization of social power, leveling down the hierarchies to the place where personal and private associational effectiveness can once again take hold—it is this way we need to move not only in our political but in our productive and everyday life-support systems.

The analysis of humiliation and self-esteem which we began in chapter 3 is not complete without this rehabilitation of the public world as publicly *available* to average human beings. And this means the revival of conviviality—personally available tools operating in a social setting shaped to the contours of self-accomplishment and innovative transaction with others and with our natural environment. Forms of self-affirmation which do not include this political referent remain a kind of in-house therapy, lobotomizing our continuing estrangement from fundamental species needs. Moreover, only by way of this experience of effectiveness can we overcome our fawning voyeurism toward the supersuccessful, our attempt to gain some kind of inner aliveness if only vicariously. Only then can we turn our attention from the prestige mongering of abstract and high-level power brokering to the rights of concrete life settings, upon which such panoplies of power always remain parasitic. Only then can we withdraw ourselves from an unhealthy dependency upon "officials" and so remove from their competency any generalized inquiry or attempted management of our self-space or private associational lives. In the end privacy depends upon this "sense of standing," a sense of inner substance and reserve which can be with itself without panic of emptiness and so enjoy the familiarity of others without requiring of them the guarantee of their secrets.

But this "sense of standing" poses the deepest problems today. For holding our own place in reality implies a kind of "religious" effectiveness, a grasp on firm horizons of meaning. And here we have had recently to wrestle most profoundly to maintain ourselves against an overpowering sense of humiliation, the humiliation not just of our personal, not just of our cultural, but also of our species significance. Never have the dimensions of reality so explosively expanded for those conscious of such things, and never has man seemed more diminished.

5

Privacy and Transcendence

If we banish man . . . the universe becomes quiet; silence and night take over. All is transformed into a vast solitude, where unobserved phenomena take place, in darkness and in deafness. It is the presence of man that renders natural existence interesting.[1]
—Diderot, *Encyclopedie*

Our struggle to hold on to a sense of significance is even more difficult because we are overwhelmed by the rapidly expanding dimensions of reality itself. We are confronted with a heightened awareness of our own finitude and our contingency in the rush of events.

Finitude

Anselm became a famous Bishop of Canterbury for thinking up one of the more fascinating "proofs" of God—namely, the ontological or argument from the nature of reality. If God exists, Anselm began, then everyone agrees He would have to be "a being than which nothing greater can be conceived." In both Eastern and Western religions the idea of divinity has traditionally been associated with notions of the highest or most powerful and excellent reality. The word "God" is one way men have tried to delimit their existence, or at least affirm that it was delimited, defining the horizons of reality. The problem today is that our premonitions of these horizons have so enormously expanded that it has left many of us not knowing what to say.

True, since Copernicus we have been persuaded that the earth is not the center of our solar system, that *we move*, not the sun. Still, in some curious way we did continue to believe—and depend upon the idea—that the earth held a central (perhaps *the* central) place in the total system of significance. As philosopher Immanuel Kant said, "I hold in awe not so much the stars but the astronomer who contemplates them." More recently, the theologian Teilhard de Chardin has sought to refine this argument. We bring to reality, he claimed, the wrong scale of measurement if we reckon by mere size or force. The process of reality—not just here on earth, but analogizing from what evolution seems to be up to this point as we understand the development of cosmic significance in general—is toward the emergence of consciousness.[2] Thus Teilhard could speak so confidently about the place of man in the overall scheme of things. But this confidence seems premature, both in terms of what we know about the nature of consciousness and what we have learned about the awesome destruction/creativity at work in the abyss of space.

Freud was frank to admit the eroding effect upon man's self-confidence of his view of the foundations in the irrational of much of our everyday activity. Consciousness is not so much a supreme director as a harassed broker in the marketplace of libidinal push and the repressive shove Freud thought necessary for civilized routine. Man's self-reflective capacities are undermined by the fact that the self which reflects upon itself is not some disinterested contemplator but a biological organism with all the complexities of such a being. Still, our view of consciousness has been humbled by not only what we have learned about the irrational but also by what we have learned about the *this-worldly, inter-human* origins of man's self-reflective capacity. Consciousness is first of all a function of our species' social nature (see chapter 3). Without human intercourse, consciousness simply *is not*. And human intercourse is *culturally relative*. We begin, it seems, as earth creatures, and rather recent arrivals at that, precariously emerging in our present form out of the catastrophes of an ice age, and of uncertain future and tenure. The net effect of recent discoveries in the sciences of man has been this self-awareness of what man really is—and (unanticipated) the loneliness of it all. We feel a strange combination of awe and humility that we should have come to be here this way—and able to know it.

But not only the way of our arrival as a species has stunned us, but also the place we now know we have arrived at. We look up at the Milky Way, our galaxy, filled with billions of sun systems like our own. Or with the aid of optical or radio telescopes we look past our galaxy into the abyss of billions of other galaxies like this one, each with its billions of suns. Billions raised to the billionth power—you can see how Anselm might feel a little vertigo.

We can watch stars being born in the gaseous regions of the Horsehead nebulae. If recent speculations prove correct about the awesome spectacle of the supernova, we may be witness to the explosive terminus not just of stars but of whole galaxies of stars. We shudder before other experiments in being long since over, their suns burned out billions of years ago and collapsed, unable to say anything to us—except precisely that they have ended. Or we grow silent in turn before those future attempts at creation we can watch just now focusing and forming themselves out of the swirling hydrogen clouds. If "holding our own ground," having a "sense of standing," is the essence of privacy, then how are we to lay hold of it these days? How can we fix the horizons and give boundaries and form to our significance? How can we keep from getting lost in reality?

Finitude lays a heavy burden upon our freedom. As creatures who construct our world by weaving into it shared meanings and systems of significance, this humbling can cause us to resent and flee so precarious a sovereignty. Diminished already, why not complete the process ourselves? With what gratitude some turn themselves over to those who relieve them of their burden of wonder, setting them adrift in mindless pleasantries or bowing before new/old-found Supremacies. Feet wandering around looking for a world to stand on—or wishing they didn't have any feet. The active self, the executive ego, this bold privacy is under attack these days not just by others, but most fundamentally by itself. And the self which belittles itself can have small sense of the awesome depths of others, or prize the boldness of that fleeting internal space which holds its ground before overwhelming external forces.

Still, the issue is not yet fully presented. Once we start trying to hold our place, we enter even more fully into our finitude.

Contingency

Hannah Arendt reflects upon those who have dared boldness and taken hold of their lives and times. They learn from their transaction with history that,

> he who acts never quite knows what he is doing, that he always becomes "guilty"
> of consequences he never intended or even foresaw, that no matter how disastrous
> and unexpected the consequences of his deed he can never undo it, that the
> process he starts is never consummated unequivocally in one single deed or event,
> and that its very meaning never discloses itself to the actor but only to the
> backward glance of the historian who himself does not act.[3]

This exposure to contingency—the power that meets our power and deflects us from the simplicity of intended goals—is greeted by rationalists and revolutionaries alike as profoundly debilitating. Both prefer conspiracy theories of history because they make "more sense" out of the things that happen here and so bolster our feeling of being effectively in charge. History eventually embitters them and they withdraw. It takes, it seems, a different kind of spirit—more generous perhaps, less suspicious of what it does not control—to dialogue with the times over the long haul.

The trouble is we are creatures who remain haunted by a need for conviction, for confidence concerning our basic competence for life. The reason is simply that we must ourselves fuel and energize our world and cannot depend upon an automatic instinctual enlivening. Without this sense of conviction we lose interest in our world, deaden our attentiveness to it, and let our focus drift. In the past one of religion's chief enterprises has been to bridge this gap between contingency and conviction and so supply society with a sense of steadiness and personal significance.

In Hinduism this was done by developing the idea of *karma*, the ineluctable moral law which moves behind the facade of time and brings to final sense that which in man's hands remains unfinished, threatening to be non-sense. This historical law of karma, combined with the idea of the soul's reincarnation and society's caste obligations, produced a logically tight scheme of significance which "handled" the problem of contingency by extending the space-time dimension beyond what we can see or know, yet without dissolving man's personal sense of effectiveness for "doing his world." Each man is responsible, even if he doesn't have a map of the whole territory. And in the cycle of incarnation each gets precisely what he morally deserves. Karma presented a persuasive drama of the soul which for centuries fueled a now ancient culture.[4]

Similar in function is Christianity's idea of Providence. This concept provides the bridge between what seems to be going on and what we need to feel about the relationship between human intentions and historical consequences in order to remain active shapers of our circumstances. Man does not live by ambiguity. Life at its everyday level is both more serious and more un-self-conscious than the delicately balanced poise of the ironic spectator. With its doctrine of Divine Providence, Christianity recognized this simple pastoral fact. It sought to shepherd men's souls into serious moral effort despite the always obvious bewilderment that "the rain falls equally on the just and the unjust." The moral opaqueness of history, it asserted, is undergirded by a hidden yet determinative Foreordination whose Will is wholly good. This doctrine vastly strengthened man's conviction for his public task and calling. In the name of humility, it birthed a boldness that shaped a whole civilization.

Nonetheless, whether karma or providence, each depended upon the persuasion of a firm floor of powerful meaning lying just beneath the shifting sands of history. Therefore each required the "intimate attention," as it were, of a corrective divine dimension. And in an age of horizonlessness it is precisely this sense of groundedness that gives way. Billions of stars raised to a galactic billionth—many of us now seem to feel more alone and in our aloneness more fully responsible than in ages where perspective upon reality was more firmly under control. But religion is not alone in not knowing what to say. Its secular equivalents have fallen into a similar inarticulateness.

Marxism began as a vigorous reclamation of man to himself, to his species' task of molding his surroundings. It was, it seemed, a proclamation of man's right to stand his ground and be his own being. "The more of himself man attributes to God," Marx argued, "the less he has left in himself."[5] Yet this proclamation of man's sovereignty, of effectively belonging to himself, maintained its confidence against the debilitation of contingency only by constructing a "science" of history, the ultimate effect of which was once again to remove man from his own agency. History holds together and makes sense for classical Marxism not in terms of personal initiative but as the inexorable unfolding of innate dialectical laws. Freedom becomes "insight into necessity," revolutionary conformity to an assured destiny. So long as people believed it, they marched as confidently to this drummer as Bunyan's pilgrim pursued his progress. But twentieth-century Marxists have largely given up on the idea that history unfolds with such logical exactitude. After all, the twentieth century just did not happen as predicted. Intellectuals not determinedly orthodox began to look elsewhere for their fundamental explanations.

One of these places, which for awhile seemed able to marshal men's energies, is what we Americans have proved so good at: namely, pragmatic problem solving. In essence it is the attempt to bracket off ultimate questions like the merely contingent connection between man's plans and his eventual arrival. This approach is a self-conscious scaling down of the dimensions of issues to those which prove in fact capable of solution. It led for a while to an enormously profitable specialization of inquiry unencumbered by man's background anxieties—a kind of all-American healthy mindedness. But clearly this couldn't last. Max Weber, who was one of the first to study this western secularizing process, foresaw also its gathering crisis. "All research in the cultural sciences in an age of specialization," he pointed out,

> once it is oriented towards a given subject matter through particular settings of problems and has established its methodological principles, will consider the analysis of the data as an end in itself. It will discontinue assessing the value of the individual facts in terms of their relationships to ultimate value-ideas. Indeed, it will lose its awareness of its ultimate rootedness in the value-ideas in general. And it is well that should be so. But there comes a moment when the atmosphere changes. The significance of the unreflectively utilized viewpoints becomes uncertain and the road is lost in the twilight. The light of the great cultural problems moves on. Then science too prepares to change its standpoint and its analytical apparatus and to view the streams of events from the heights of thought. It follows those stars which alone are able to give meaning and direction to its labors.[6]

My contention is that we have arrived at such a point. Modern man, alert to his situation, has become a kind of burned-over territory. Prior enthusiasms in their departure have left him stunned, lacking basic conviction, wandering and self-indulgent. He has lost trust in the ultimate dignity of his inner space. I hold that this is a more accurate and important religious truth about our times than recent revivals of new and old pietisms: Jesus followers, occultism, astrology, personal-growth movements, and so on. The heart of the study of religion remains *constructive theology*. Here is where religion gets most serious about itself. And theology is mostly silent these days. We have not yet rediscovered *how to order the horizons*. What we must learn, then, is to wait without foolishness. And this means that our need for confidence about our personal significance must look less to belief—which implies a certain firmness of impression—than to the resources of courage.

Courage

The place to begin is with the self's irreducible identity with itself—that the self-recognition "I am I" cannot be converted to something else more basic. Of course much *about* ourselves can be reduced to something behind it. That I have a certain kind of visage, susceptibility to certain diseases, that I have certain deep-seated attitudes towards authority, or intimacy, or tidiness—all this can be traced to my parents' genetic or emotional endowment. Even the fact that I think this way about privacy, with these general tools of analysis and types of conceptualization, is due mostly to the fact that I am a twentieth-century American thinker who has been trained in certain theological and ethical traditions by particular teachers. In all these respects that which appears to be mine, that which seems to be "me" or actions of my self-space, can be reduced to functions of other places and processes external to the place I hold as "I." Even the musing of my spirit, its sense of vertigo before indeterminately retreating horizons, its awe before the immensity of reality, is due in large measure to the general career of the spirit among my particular companions in this time and place—the teachings, art, music, revelations that have grasped and spoken to us and for us. Biologically, intellectually, even religiously, my "I" finds itself repeatedly emptied out into its contingent externalities. I am taken away from myself, deprived of fundamental privacy.

But what cannot be reduced finally is the fact that it is "I" who am coincident with these multiple conditionings, that it is "I" who reflects upon and knows myself in this way. This is what one philosopher refers to as the "radical thrownness" of existence— that I should be this "I," here and now in this way. Theologian H. Richard Niebuhr has a fine sense for this.

> The radical action by which I am and by which I am present with this body, this mind, this emotional equipment, this religion, is not identifiable with any of the finite actions that constitute the particular elements in physical, mental, personal existence.[7]

That "I am I" is my essential mystery, the certification of the right to be who I am. Such an awareness provides an absoluteness to the privacy of our inner space. We come to know ourselves as a kind of proud embarrassment, the firm point where we turn back upon the external immensity and begin to ask about its meaning *for us.*

Now it is true that Diderot seems surely to have overspoken. It looks highly likely that he granted us too much uniqueness in assigning us the sole place in the universe where nature turns back upon itself. It seems thoroughly probable that other experiments in conscious existence lie out there, beyond our reach, among the galaxies. Still, Diderot did have a key element of truth. And that is that we are indeed *one of those places* (called freedom) where the natural process departs its immediacy, begins to ponder the meaning of its evolution and even to alter the process of its mindless unfolding. Moreover, this reflective activity characterizes us not just as a species. *Each one individually* is where nature begins to consider itself and so becomes interesting. Even when corrupted into fetishisms of ownership or of the spirit, the very fact that we are corruptible is interesting. Each of us carries this indestructible value, valuable even when turned against itself.

"I am who I am" provides a floor to my existence, a center even when the horizons are not fixed, a place for courage to take hold. We may call it *the courage to be.* Yet this courage to be requires also the courage to be *as self-transcending beings.* Why?

Transcendence and Society

Anthropologist Ernest Becker put it nicely. Observing that man is the only animal not instinctually "built into" his world, Becker pointed out,

> Evolution has . . . sealed the animal firmly into its adaptational mold. Man alone among the animals gradually develops his own perceptual response world by means of imaginative guiding concepts . . . continually creating his own reality. . . . *Other animals seem to be condemned to experience the same world for all time.*[8]

Precisely this is what requires courage—that we are constantly making and remaking our "world" as a believable and worthwhile place to live in. We are always in motion—although we usually hide the fact from ourselves—between the world that was persuasive yesterday and the one that must win our attention today. We can lose heart, find what once absorbed us no longer worth our energy. Thus man *takes into himself* the fact of finitude. It is not simply something that *happens to us* from outside. It is something *we do*. We outdistance our prior meanings.

This quest is what attracts us to the stars. We cannot leave blank spaces in our vision. We must invest them with meaning. This is the driving force behind astrology. It is the attempt to get the galaxies to speak with a humanly meaningful voice. Unfortunately, a premature rendition of significance often reduces and trivializes cosmic immensity to the dimensions of human security needs. It secures us against the invitation of the spirit's indeterminate exploration of awe.

We hold our place in reality as creatures driven ever beyond themselves toward more comprehensive and inclusive horizons of meaning. Man knows, said philosopher William James, "that he must vote always for the richer universe, for the good which seems most organizable, most fit to enter into complex combinations, most apt to be a member of a more inclusive whole. . . ." [9] But this is not easy. It requires the risk of giving up the place we have already learned to hold as our own ground. Harvard psychologist Charles Hamden-Turner sees this. "By suspending and risking his personal synthesis [man] *evokes in himself continual imitations and intimations of death,* but he does this in the name of life." [10] The courage to be is the courage to affirm oneself despite all that denies oneself, including the necessary "self-denial" by which we transgress and transcend past persuasions of our solidity and significance. For example, one of the most puzzling features of morally serious divorce is that we should have become so different from that self which first made its promise.

This internal process by which we become the active instruments of our own finitude, *the relativizers of ourselves,* is the deepest part of courage. The self in its most awesome validity exercises its right to inflict a kind of death upon itself in order to live. And this growth of ourselves *as selves* places us in fundamental tension with society's need for stable meanings and predictable enthusiasm.

Only here can we begin to glimpse the depth of tension between the rights of personal privacy and the commercial and political interests of the state. Put simply, we do not belong to the state or to the marketplace, although we can temporarily surrender to them. However unwillingly, we belong finally to ourselves. The finitude, the passing parade not only of all external spaces but of our internal syntheses of meaning, reminds us of our ultimate character as pilgrims, seekers ever of a New Jerusalem. This tension between selfhood and society is only heightened in a nation (such as ours) which in principle recognizes and even honors this fact; for such principles enter into the everyday pursuit of *legitimacy* where they remain potentially subversive of established claims to authority. This tension underlies the historic ambiguity in the West of all transactions between church and state.

Christianity first institutionalized itself outside of the political order. The later Constantinian settlement never overcame this primordial fact. Two potentially rival legitimacies, each with its own internal institutional resources, were set loose across our Western history. It is not necessary to review here this drama of the scepter and the orb—the symbols of these usually reinforcing but occasionally rival authorities. We do need, however, to note the inner structure of their discourse. For if I am correct about what is happening in Western religion today—that it has lost its horizons and so undertaken a new pilgrimage—then religion is both weaker internally and externally more dangerous than the state is likely passively to abide. The state will try to stifle this disturber of normal public comfort.

The structure of intercourse between church and state is founded upon the common-sense observation, perceived by the simplist patriot, that the political meaning of life is insufficiently meaningful, that it needs a higher blessing, a more fundamental authority. This need points to a transcendent aspect in all successful claims to legitimacy. Political-scientist John Scharr remarks upon this. "All theories of legitimacy take the form of establishing a principle which, while it resides outside power and is independent of it, locates or embeds power in a realm of things beyond the wills of the holders of power."[11] This transcendent aspect has to do with the fundamental meanings of the society in question, the basic "stories" that make sense of what human beings do and have done to them there. Persuasive leadership, as distinguished from coercion or dissembling, can exist only where there is a *coperformance of meanings* between the leaders and the led. There is this inevitable "religious" dimension to the pursuit of effective authority, and it creates an interesting dialectic between power and prestige.

The usual function of religion in this respect has clearly been conservative. It has attempted to conserve man's sense of firmly established values and mores. It has sought to consolidate and confirm man's everyday attentiveness to the "doing" of his public life, "playing its play" with full seriousness. To this end religion blesses society and its leaders, and so emboldens it with the conviction of correctness and significance. It is society's source of fundamental enthusiasm. Knowing this, political leaders have traditionally sought, if not control of, at least assured alliance with, important religious figures—whether pope or popular evangelist. Thus, while theologians periodically wax cynical about the cultural importance of religion, politicians have acted routinely upon the opposite assumption. They have paid their pew fees regularly.

But throughout Western history religion has displayed a second and quite different feature. It has been one of the bearers of man's sense of the holy, what one author has called "the *mysterium tremendum*," the sense of the awesome and overpowering mystery of reality. Indeed, out of this reservoir of the numinous—its dread, its fascinating power—the political function of religion borrows its vitality. You can see it is a heady and unstable brew to have to depend upon. Religion can simply wander away from its public responsibilities. It can follow the impulse of its primordial rootedness in transcendence, enfeebling established public meanings as it restlessly pursues a sense of significance into more distant visions. Which is to say, religious leaders may be tamed to public purposes, but religion itself has an intensely private life of its own—an undisciplined interior vitality which disdains subservience to society's ambitions—"these dignities," quipped Saint Augustine, "that totter on these shifting sands." This is religion deadly serious about itself. Not something we do because it makes us feel good but something that haunts and pursues us, not so much secure comfort as indeterminate fascination. It follows that the state has an obvious interest in imposing itself upon this "private intensity" and so reducing its unpredictability. Especially is this the case when institutionalized religion begins not simply to confirm but vocally to oppose the mundane order in the name of a higher allegiance. If sustained, this tension becomes a fundamental struggle over the definition of "citizenship" in which either the holders of religious or of political office are likely to become resident aliens vis-à-vis their own institutional base.

Privacy and the Church

Moved by this memory, the church—as an institution of authority within an institution of authority (the state)—has learned to be continuously alert to issues of its own privacy: the integrity of its financial and membership records, the seclusion of its internal discussions and decisions, the protected relationship between pastor and communicant, the publically unsupervised education of its clergy. The church has viewed itself as "within" the state—and therefore subject to its jurisdiction—in only a very limited sense. Proclaiming itself (and upon occasion even evidencing the idea) as representative of an *inclusive commonwealth* of *reality* in which nations hold but a passing place, the church has time and again become the target of political leaders seeking to consolidate their authority. We find examples of this in our own time in the attempt by government to tame church and synagogue to proper "civil obedience." I have in mind the demonstrated availability to government officials of church bank records, and the legally precarious protection of the priest-penitent relationship.[12]

The Unitarian-Universalist Association and the Boston Grand Jury

When a federal grand jury in Boston was investigating the alleged theft and subsequent publication of the *Pentagon Papers*, it sent FBI operatives to examine the bank records of Beacon Press. Beacon Press had published the so-called "Gravel edition" of those papers. Five days after the volumes came out, agents appeared at the New England Merchants National Bank asking for all financial records of Beacon Press and its parent body, the Unitarian-Universalist Association. The bank at first refused, requesting a court subpoena. The next day the grand jury issued such a subpoena. It called for copies of all checks drawn out and all checks deposited in Unitarian-Universalist accounts between June 1 and October 15, 1971. The subpoena was served on the bank on October 29, and FBI agents began working with bank employees in going through the church's records.

The church was given no notice by the bank of what was happening. Indeed, it was six days later, on November 4, that the Unitarians learned that the FBI was examining its denominational accounts. Meanwhile, a decision by the U.S. Court of Appeals had halted all investigation until it ruled on the extent of Senator Gravel's immunity under the Constitution. The government was quick to indicate, however, that it would resume its investigation when that issue was settled. In response the Unitarians went to court to challenge any such examination of their bank records on the grounds of governmental interference with the free exercise of religion, as well as freedom of association and freedom of the press.

But according to Alexander Hoffman, vice-president of Double-day, this kind of threat to the privacy of religious association had *already* had a "chilling effect" upon the Unitarian Church.[13] Contributions diminished. Some contributors asked that their names and addresses be expunged from the records as past contributors. Indeed, members even wrote to Beacon Press asking if their names would appear on FBI lists as a result of past or prospective purchases of the *Pentagon Papers*. Employees of the Unitarian-Universalist Association became uneasy about their status in the eyes of government and of the public. Some left their jobs and potential new employees proved reluctant to apply.

By this invasion of the reserve of the church's associational life government had successfully exacted a high price from the Unitarians for their political boldness. Those familiar with the field are aware, however, that the ultimate federal weapon in all this is the power to remove the church's tax shelter because of so-called "excessive involvement" in politics. The Internal Revenue Service has been in continuous struggle with the National Council of Churches on just this issue. Federal officials deny any intended intimidation. But intentions aside, the actual effect is obvious— and ominous. Indeed, in some cases the official denial is patently hollow. Take, for example, a memo sent in September, 1970, by White House aide Tom Huston to H. R. Haldeman, at that time Nixon's chief of staff. It read in part:

> Nearly eighteen months ago, the President indicated a desire for IRS to move against leftist organizations taking advantage of tax shelters. . . . What we cannot do in a courtroom via criminal prosecutions to curtail the activities of some of these groups, IRS could do by administrative action.[14]

Irrespective of how the particular controversy over the *Pentagon Papers* turned out, the incident with the Unitarians aroused interest by a number of organizations which have been routinely relying upon their banks to protect the confidentiality of their financial records. The American Civil Liberties Union, for example, wrote to the presidents of the one hundred largest banks in the country, asking their policy in responding to requests by governmental investigators to examine the bank records of subject depositors. The replies indicated that most major banks do require a subpoena or court order before complying. Also, the Unitarians have now obtained from their banks an agreement not to divulge financial information without notifying them in sufficient time to go into court to attempt to quash the subpoena. The National Council of Churches has obtained a similar agreement of prior notification.

However, some banks do not notify a subject depositor that his records are being examined *even after the fact*. This is more likely to be the case for those with less public standing than religious denominations. Take the example of the National Black Economic Development Conference of Chester, Pennsylvania. One of the Media FBI files relates the following:

> On 5/20/70, Mr. Daniel McGronigle, Cashier, Southeast National Bank (formerly Delaware County National Bank), 4th and Market Streets, Chester, Pa., advised that as of 1/1/70 the Delaware County National Bank merged with several Chester County banks to form the Southeast National Bank. Subsequent to this merger, this bank instituted a new computer system for checking accounts. Under this system all checks drawn on active checking accounts are recorded on microfilm and available for review at the Computer Center of this bank at 24th and Edgmont Avenue, Chester, Pa.

> On 5/20/70, Mr. Allan Ferguson, Executive Officer, Computer Center, Southeast National Bank . . . made available for review copies of the statement for checking account #550-723-1, which is in the name National Black Economic Development Conference, Pennsylvania Office.[15]

Here the bank permitted access to records without either subpoena or subsequent depositor notification.

Given the widely varying practices by banks, Senators Tunney of California and Mathias of Maryland have introduced two amendments to the Bank Secrecy Act (viz., Senate Bills 3814 and 3828) that would prohibit banks from divulging depositors' records except under one of three conditions: (1) prior notification of the depositor and the obtaining of his consent, (2) reception of a subpoena, or (3) a court order resulting from a "probable cause" hearing similar to that required for a search warrant. Unfortunately, although hearings were held by Senator Proxmire's Subcommittee on Financial Institutions, no legislation had been passed as of the end of the 1973 session.

Dean Kelley, head of the civil and religious liberties division of the National Council of Churches, points out that,

> It should not be necessary to resort to clandestine meetings, secret passwords and vows of silence in order to protect the collective right of privacy of organizational life. Organizations and their members should be able to expect that their records and correspondence are confidential, that they are not infiltrated by spies and provocateurs, and that their premises are not invaded by electronic or other devices for eavesdropping or surveillance.[16]

The truth is that none of this can presently be taken for granted. Even the church has become suspect. To be sure, such suspicion is age-old. The state has always looked rather suspiciously at the church, especially its upper ecclesiastics, as possessed by ambition to preside not just over heaven but over earth as well. And sometimes it has been so. But hardly today. For the foreseeable future the church will be in a minority position vis-à-vis the everyday panoply of the state, especially given citizen dependency upon the new administrative state. Moreover, transcendence is counter to the efficiency of executive control. It complicates citizenship with unwholesome second thoughts about another and better homeland. As a result, the church will have to fight doggedly for its privacy if it is to preserve its own inner integrity. An example of this is the present precariousness in law of the priest-penitent relationship. Most people think (wrongly as it turns out) that it enjoys an absolute protection.

The confidentiality between pastor and communicant

To begin with we should note that the privilege for clergymen rests upon statute rather than common law. In the absence of specific statutory protection the clergyman can be compelled to testify in court under penalty of imprisonment for contempt if he refuses.[17] In the U.S.A. there are six states which have no statutory privilege for clergymen: Alabama, Connecticut, Mississippi, New Hampshire, Texas, and West Virginia. Twenty-three states have a "limited and questionable privilege" patterned after what has come to be known as the "traditional statute" of New York dating from 1828. Its relevant section reads as follows: "No minister of the gospel, or priest of any denomination whatsoever shall be allowed to disclose any confessions made to him in his professional character, in the course of discipline enjoined by the rules of practice of such denomination" (New York Revised Statutes,

3872). To qualify for this privilege, a communication must meet four tests:

1. It must be made to a *clergyman*. (A nun in New Jersey claimed the privilege recently, but the court said she wasn't entitled.)

2. It must be a *"confession."*

3. It must be made to the clergyman in his *professional character.*

4. It must be made in the "course of discipline enjoined by the rules of practice" of the clergyman's (and penitent's) denomination.

Obviously, the so-called "traditional statute" does not afford much protection. Not many communications can in practice qualify under its terms. In fact the terms themselves are so ambiguous as to leave a clergyman almost wholly uncertain of just where he stands legally. Should he, for example, permit a husband to continue a conversation if as a clergyman he suspects he might be called as a witness in a divorce case? Indeed, more courts have ruled adversely than favorably on the claim of privilege under the traditional statute. Such courts decided either the communication was not a "confession," or the individual was not acting in his "professional capacity," or the individual was not a "minister," or it was not in the course of the discipline of his church, or the penitent was not a member of that church, or the clergyman was acting only as a marriage counselor, or he was obliged to testify to observations he made at the time even if not to content of the confidential communication itself. Put simply, the traditional statute *does not protect.*

Recognizing this, twenty-one states as well as the District of Columbia have broadened the privilege. The states are:

California	Kansas	New Mexico
Delaware	Louisiana	New York
Virginia	Maryland	North Carolina
Florida	Massachusetts	Pennsylvania
Georgia	Minnesota	Rhode Island
Illinois	Nebraska	South Carolina
Iowa	New Jersey	Tennessee

These no longer confine the protected communication to a "confession." They have broadened it to include any "confidence" or "information" imparted to a clergyman in the course of his professional practice as spiritual advisor or counselor, whether by a member of his church or not. Yet even these broader statutes do not guarantee that the clergyman will not be compelled to testify. Again there are more decisions under these newer statutes denying the privilege than granting it.

One should note that there is no federal statute concerning this issue at all. There are two federal decisions which seem to give precedent for granting it. The more recent case *(Mullen* v. *U.S.,* 1958) lays a foundation which seems solid. It argues that

> The benefit of preserving these confidences inviolate overbalances the possible benefit of permitting litigation to prosper at the expense of the tranquility of the home, the integrity of the professional relationship and the spiritual rehabilitation of a penitent.[18]

Still this is uncertain of future application.

In face of this disarray, a recent law-review article which thoroughly surveys the situation makes this recommendation concerning the wording of a model code.

> If any person shall communicate with a clergyman in his professional capacity and in a confidential manner (i) to make a confession, (ii) to seek spiritual counsel or comfort or (iii) to enlist help in connection with a marital problem, either such person or the clergyman shall have the privilege, in any legal or quasi-legal proceeding, to refuse to disclose and to prevent the other party from disclosing anything said by either party during such communication.[19]

But the situation which presently bears upon clergymen and laymen remains far from this model protection. An impartial summary of the situation would have to conclude:

1. That most purported "confidences" between clergyman and counselees *are not protected* by existing statutes and precedents from being divulged in court;

2. That most uninstructed clergymen and laymen (and the best known books on the subject, like the *Minister's Law Handbook or The Right to Silence* by W. H. Tremann) purport the clergy to be privileged when probably they are not.

3. That better statutes need enacting.

4. That clergymen and counselors who want their confidences
   protected should take care to meet at least the minimum
   requirements—*(a)* that it not be casual or informal encounter
   but a serious spiritual exercise, and *(b)* that it not be overheard
   by a third party or recorded without consent or divulged to
   anyone else thereafter.

Having taken all these precautions, let the clergyman still be
warned that the precedent of court decisions is mostly negative as
regards protection, and the precedents are exceedingly narrow as to
the definition of privileged communications. Contrary to most
people's assumption, their minister's, priest's, or rabbi's study is
far from being legally sheltered from compulsory revelation. In
terms of law, the door is open for the state to enter that study more
rather than less at will. Nor is it at all evident that public opinion
will restrain the state as regards the privacy and freedom of
religious association. Like so many other things, it seems a matter
of public taste—or better, of public antipathy.

De-programming Transcendence

A thirty-one-year-old woman is kidnapped from the streets of
Manhattan and taken into New Jersey. The police discover that her
estranged husband, whom she had left several months earlier to
join a fundamentalistic religious fellowship, had hired a man by
the name of Ted Patrick to do the job. The "job" Patrick does is as a
self-styled expert in religious de-conversion. He saves people from
being saved. Presented with incontrovertible evidence of the
kidnap charge, a New York grand jury nevertheless refused to
indict. The rights of free religious association belong evidently
only to routine religions and those who are routinely religious.
Anything more total represents a subversion of certified spirituali-
ty, a candidate for therapeutic reconditioning.

The same Mr. Patrick was recently the subject of a national TV
documentary. It showed him kidnapping a California woman in
her early twenties on instruction of her parents. As a teenager she
had gotten into drugs and sexual promiscuity until she fled from
her mounting degradations into a puritanically strict, millen-
nialist, religious commune. The documentary showed that even
with advance knowledge and a direct appeal by the young
woman—who was clearly both of age and mentally competent—

the police systematically refused to intervene in the kidnap. Reprogramming unwanted transcendence is protected it seems by portions of "adult" society even when it involves blatantly illegal means.

Religion as the bearer of the sense of the numinous, religion in its private, unprogrammed, and incalculable self-identity, represents a force which those who are already terrified by the dark outside their small corner of light wish profoundly to be removed. Religion as the courage to be oneself, as the courage to transcend, surrenders to the established world of significance—*Glamour,* "making it," "doctor," all-American healthy mindedness, and football—religion, as living spirit, many would see dead. For to live means to be alive in a life that is alive. Fleeing that we flee the homeland of transcendence for the mirage of finality. We muzzle inner space and reduce ourselves to a surpriseless appearance of things.

Privacy, boldness of self-space, the "looked at" which dares look back is a matter in part of political and commercial practice. In the next chapter I shall make suggestions for correctives in these practices. But in the end privacy is a matter of the spirit, the courage of the spirit in face of the coercions and seductions of outer space to undertake its own journey. Because *we are,* we must therefore dare to be *our own story*—unique, never to be repeated, our own best remembrance. It is this sense of inner immensity in which privacy takes hold.

6

Private Man
and
Public World

The overall argument I have been trying to make is that we are faced with two complementary pressures which together threaten to unravel our heritage of freedom. These are (1) the invasion of personal privacy for the sake of commercial or political advantage and (2) the privatizing of effective public power in the hands of a highly benefited minority. We turn now to what we can do, practically speaking, both as individuals and as members of private associations to reverse this process, keeping private spaces private while making public ones once again publicly available; hence, the title of this final chapter, "Private Man and Public World." First, protecting private man—

Protecting Privacy

"'Tis so," said the Duchess: "and the moral of that is—
Oh, 'tis love that makes the world go round!"
"Somebody said," Alice whispered, "that it's done by everybody minding their own business."
—Lewis Carroll, *Alice's Adventures in Wonderland*

From the earliest days of the nation the invasion of privacy was in practice well established. A visit to almost any of the great colonial mansions will reveal specially constructed listening places, hidden from the untutored eye, where faithful servants would be posted to collect the whispered comments of unsuspecting business rivals. Industrial espionage is as old in this country as industry itself. Needless to say, its efficiency has been vastly increased by the centralization of business records in remote access, time-shared computers. Similarly, the attempt to use law to invade and coerce private conscience is at least as old as the Alien and Sedition Acts of 1798. By means of these acts the Federalists attempted, rather successfully, to suppress the dissenting opinion of Republicans, and for a while threatened with jail both Thomas Jefferson and Thomas Paine. The ambition, once again, is old but recently made easier by high-technology snooping and a revolution in the communications media which makes the mass marketing of political image so potent. As regards privacy, we have reached then a crucial turning point in our practice of commerce and politics and, more immediately, in the evolution of American law. It is to this legal issue that I turn next.

Privacy in American law[1]

There is no "right" to privacy specifically mentioned in either the Constitution or the Bill of Rights. True, portions of the Bill of Rights were drafted in direct response to certain practices by the English overlords that amounted to invasions of privacy. As a result, it is possible to argue along with Professor Emerson of Yale Law School that a right to privacy seems to be inferred in our nation's founding documents. The First Amendment, for example, prohibits government scrutiny of political expression and association. The Third Amendment prohibits the then hated practice of invading private homes for the quartering of troops. The Fourth Amendment prevents general searches, which had so terrified the colonists and kept their political associations constantly off balance. The Fifth Amendment prohibits government from compelling persons to make revelations which could be used to incriminate them in court. But beyond this, little in that early period indicates a specific interest in a more general "right" to privacy. In fact common practice seemed often enough to move in the opposite direction.

As time went along, there were a number of well-known assertions concerning the right of privacy by significant figures in the American legal tradition. Judge Story, for example, wrote in 1841 of the violation of correspondence that it "strikes at the root of all that free and mutual interchange of advice, opinions, and sentiments [that] is so essential to the well-being of society."[2] Given our recent law-and-order preoccupations, Judge Thomas

Cooley was even more to the point in his *Constitutional Limitations* of 1868. He argued that

> [It] is better sometimes that crime should go unpunished than that the citizen should be liable to have his premises invaded, his desks broken open, his private books, letters and papers exposed to prying curiosity, and to the misconstructions of ignorant and suspicious persons.[3]

However, it was really only in 1890, in a now famous *Harvard Law Review* article by Warren and Brandeis, that a full-fledged argument was made for privacy as a "right" inherent in our basic legal commitments. Warren and Brandeis wrote that the common law "secures to each individual the right of determining, ordinarily, to what extent his thoughts, sentiments, and emotions shall be communicated to others."[4] But this remained a narrowly based concept, having mostly to do with the use of personal information by prying newspaper columnists. From this beginning has developed the recognition by a majority of states of a certain *common-law* right to privacy having to do with the use, without consent, of one's name or likeness for advertising purposes.

The wider truth seems to be that the development in American law of the concept of a general right to privacy, protected by the Constitution, is still underway. The Supreme Court, for example, has so far refused to hold that the Constitution contains a comprehensive "right to privacy," defined broadly as "the right to be left alone." However, the Court has taken a number of important steps in that direction. As Professor Westin points out in *Data Banks in a Free Society:* "In the course of protecting some explicitly stated Constitutional rights, the Supreme Court has given protection over the past decades to many important 'components' of the rights to privacy."[5]

One of these components is the protection against improper government wiretapping based on the Fourth Amendment. Still, those expert in the field are persuaded that vast numbers of illegal wiretaps continue to be placed almost routinely. Justice Douglas, in fact, recently stated that he was "morally certain" that the sacrosanct Conference Room of the Supreme Court itself had been bugged. Or again, the Fifth Amendment has been used to bar physical or psychological intrusions into a person's mind or body, but is not as yet applied to commercial advertising. The First Amendment has been held to guarantee the right to publish and distribute anonymous leaflets, the right to resist compulsory disclosure of membership lists, and the right to withhold information about individual beliefs and associations from compulsory disclosure. But the "clearing operations" that took place in such cities as Philadelphia before a recent presidential visit, where pickets were arrested and a judge's order defied, reveal the precariousness of this guarantee. Moreover, during the 1950s and 1960s there were *no* Supreme Court cases upholding a person's right to withhold information from executive agencies on grounds of an individual's right to privacy, for example, from use in government programs such as the decennial census. Our lives remain in this regard mostly an open book.

True, in the landmark case of *Griswold* v. *Connecticut* (1965) involving that state's controversial anti-birth-control law, the Supreme Court held that the specific guarantees in the Bill of Rights establish "zones of privacy."[6] Or as Justice Goldberg argued in a concurring opinion, the Fourteenth Amendment's due-process clause protects those rights "so rooted in the traditions and conscience of our people as to be ranked as fundamental."[7] Nevertheless, just a year later in *Katz* v. *United States* the Court specifically stated that it was not setting down some general right to privacy and that this must be left to the initiative of the individual states. With the revelations of Watergate continuing to pile up, however, the Court may conclude that it was overly sanguine as regards actions at the federal level which threaten privacy, and as a result became more bold in its position.

In sum, our present situation seems to be that there is a general need for privacy without a corresponding general or comprehensive legal right of privacy. There is a beachhead established in American law, but no more than that.

This seems especially the case if we turn from personal privacy to examine the question of *associational reserve*. The importance of protected associations is well stated by Professor Westin.

> Privacy is a necessary element for the protection of organizational autonomy, gathering of information and advice, preparation of positions, internal decision making, inter-organizational negotiations, and timing of disclosure.[8]

This issue has been approached by the Court beginning with *NAACP* v. *Alabama* (1958) and continuing in a series of NAACP cases. Less forthright than the *Griswold* decision, the Supreme

Court nonetheless recognized that voluntary communities "need breathing space to survive," and "particularly where a group espouses dissident beliefs."[9] Important new ground was opened up in this regard in a 1972 case involving political surveillance. In *United States* v. *U.S. District Court for the Eastern District of Michigan* the Court argued:

> intelligence gathering . . . risks infringement of constitutional protected privacy of speech. Security surveillance is especially sensitive because of the inherent vagueness of the domestic security concept, the necessarily broad and continuing nature of intelligence gathering, and the temptation to utilize such surveillance to oversee political dissent.[10]

But in a case decided that same year (*Laird* v. *Tatum*), the log jam in this whole area was clearly revealed. Arlo Tatum of the American Friends (Quaker) Service Committee sought a court injunction prohibiting army surveillance of lawful civilian political activity on the grounds that it produced a "chilling effect" on their First Amendment rights. The secretary of defense responded that disturbances in the nation's cities justified the army's gathering of data to enable it to respond effectively to future domestic outbreaks. Posed with this issue, the Court decided that Tatum lacked standing to sue because claim to a "subjective chill" was insufficient to provide court jurisdiction. A majority of the Court held that a citizen must show that the surveillance constituted "present harm" or the "threat of a specific future harm." The practical effect of this has been that governmental agencies—both federal and local—need no prior judicial approval, nor need they show "probable cause" to believe that the surveilled subject is engaged or about to engage in criminal conduct. In effect, the doors have swung wide open. This lack of judicial relief from unwarranted invasion of associational activity needs immediate congressional attention.

We are brought then to the present moment, where a broader constitutional right to privacy seems to be emerging but not yet fully established. We find ourselves in a period of rapidly growing public and private capacity, incentive, and willingness to invade our personal and group privacy, with the only slowly evolving notion of a generalized right to privacy to protect us. This juxtaposition makes ours a critical period of legal and administrative initiative regarding the quality of personal reserve and freedom in our nation. Specific suggestions for the development of legislation, together with professional codes of ethics to protect privacy are listed later in this chapter. But first we must make the case for a *statutory approach* to the protection of privacy, an approach some scholars shun.

A statutory approach to protecting privacy

Some experts fear a statutory approach to greater privacy protection because it might, as they say, "open up the Bill of Rights." But their assumption that we already enjoy sufficient standing in law for a firm claim to individual and group privacy seems belied by the hesitant groping of recent Court decisions. I am persuaded, therefore, that the particular suggestions for guarding privacy cited below need to be incorporated within a comprehensive statutory definition and protection of privacy. There are difficulties in framing such an approach with the necessary precision. But the attempt seems warranted, because the present case-by-case development is too slow to keep pace with speeding technological advances and too dependent upon what individual judges make of hazy concepts like an "inherent right to privacy." In order for the principles which make up that right to be effective, they need to be interrelated across the entire experience of living in a complex society and unified from that perspective. Put simply, for privacy to take genuine hold in our society there must be a *system of privacy protection.*

Moreover, the public process of framing such a statute would help overcome an inherent danger in the development of law by court decisions alone. We already feel that our lives are too much managed by distant elites conversing in specialized languages. It would be ironic indeed if the right to privacy which is meant to enhance man's independence—the dignity, so to speak, of his "self-legislated places"—was handed to him as *someone else's private decision* over his privacy. Furthermore, a tough hammering out of the issues in public debate would give impetus to a more compatible system of privacy legislation at both the federal and state levels, and lend greater uniformity between the several states.

Finally, and perhaps most important, I am convinced that public attention directed at this time to the rights of privacy would give a renewed sense of individual dignity and independence to a citizenry that often feels cowed and overwhelmed by the giantism of modern society. It could provide occasion to reexperience something of the exhilaration of a "declaration of independence." Accepting the attendant dangers of emotionalism and posturing, I would trust the legislative process of compromise to prove in the end the best forum for the development of a legal concept of privacy. For privacy is itself necessarily a compromise between institutional needs for acquiring, storing, and retrieving information and the individual's need for seclusion.

The general guidelines for such legislation seem clear.

1. Decisions concerning information systems and the protection of privacy must be located in a wider arena of discourse than internal organizational settings, with their built-in preoccupation with efficiency and cost effectiveness. This means, in turn, that:

2. The legal tradition of our country which assumes that information-gathering issues are simply internal, corporate, or agency questions needs to be brought up-to-date in terms of the public impact of those practices.

3. Far more attention must be paid not only to the citizen's right of access, but also to the avoidance of all unnecessary sharing of data by compartmentalizing confidential information stored in computerized or large manual data banks whether business or government.

4. More careful concern must be given to the *dangers* of gathering personal or group information, however service oriented the original intention. A new sense of "you have no right to ask that" needs to be defined and encouraged.

Failure to take affirmative action now to guard privacy can lead to only two results: a totally controlled and administered society, or a human revolt and reversion to particularism which vastly undermines the civilizing potentials of a more complex and comprehensive society. It is not suggested that the specific proposals for legislative and administrative action which follow are exhaustive, or even anticipate many of the problems. I would like to think, however, that these suggestions will provoke a much-needed dialogue between citizens and the commercial-governmental bureaucracies which claim to serve them.

Personal data systems

Large data banks of personal information with all their attendant dangers to human freedom seem to be inevitable. Yet the coming of the computer society does not have to mean adopting a pessimistic acceptance of the loss of privacy and autonomy. Just as the computer has the capacity to dehumanize, so it has the capacity to be a liberating force in our society. The decisions as to which direction we will go will be made soon. But it is a scene of *human decision,* not one of machine inevitability. Similarly, bureaucracy need not mean closed hierarchies and loss of citizen participation. In fact there is evidence that a strong bureaucracy, with broad humanistic values, can *protect* the exercise of freedom from the ambitions of centralized executive interests (the White House, for example, or a mayor's office) to absorb all effective decision making into itself. This is an issue we will speak to at greater length later in this chapter. But it is important to note it here. For it is upon the twin foundations of the potential humanizing effect of high-technology information systems and bureaucratic practice sensitive to the fact that its *object* of commercial or social service is in turn (and more importantly) a *human subject,* that I propose my specific recommendations for legislation.

A relatively recent issue of *Business Week* reported the establishment of a nationwide "data inspection board" in Sweden, with full licensing power to oversee all commercial data banks.[11] Sweden means to include in this any computerized listing that identifies people, such as payroll records, membership rolls, mailing services, credit and bank records, and so on. The law provides that individuals may see their files, arrange for correction if incorrect, and *sue for damages* if the misinformation harmed them. In our country Representative Barry Goldwater, Jr., has introduced legislation, "Fair Personal Information Practice," which contains many of these same features, although without the crucial licensing provisions. Add the licensing function, together with a strong clause on the right to sue for damages, and I believe we gain an effective focus for the *full statutory debate on privacy* I have urged above.

Such a "National Data Control Board" should have free access to all commercial, educational, and medical (excluding psychiatric and counseling) data banks or large manual systems. Because of the sensitive nature of such records to industrial espionage or political or law-enforcement misuse, the board should be composed of distinguished citizens who have thoroughly divested themselves of possible conflicts of interest and should operate with assured independence from other government agencies or offices. For example, the Internal Revenue Service or various law-enforcement agencies should not look to a "National Data Control Board" as an investigative source. Because such a review board carries potential for dangerous misuse, appropriate safeguards are vital.

A "National Data Control Board" should determine how each type and class of data bank may be used and what methods it may employ. In this process it must be careful to protect the industrial security of rival computer systems and their technological innovations. The following general rules are suggested for the overall guidance of a control board, and should be included in its enabling legislation.

Access. Individuals listed in a data bank are to be entitled to free printouts of their files in readable form. The board may order a data-bank operator to give notification to the data subject of his inclusion. Persons may petition the board for correction or expungement of a file and may sue for damages if misinformation has harmed them. No informal access by other government officials shall be permitted. Access shall be by customer authorization or by subpoena (usually with prior customer notification and opportunity to challenge) or by search warrant (normally with inventory of information taken).

Personally Sensitive Information. No data bank may list criminal records, psychiatric treatment, alcohol or drug abuse, or other sensitive data except with the permission of the board. Access to raw test data (as in psychological or behavioral testing) should be restricted to highly trained professionals. And the material should not be maintained, without reevaluation, beyond carefully set time limits. Test evaluations should not be used beyond the specific purpose for which the exam was originally given without subject authorization. Computerization of sensitive personal data should not be undertaken in the absence of a clear need to do so that outweighs the right of privacy. Only certain organizations should be permitted to solicit specified types of personally sensitive information, and only then for sufficient reason and, except in the rarest occasions, with the informed consent of the questioned person.

Networking. Boundaries to data sharing and networking should be developed with special attention to the rights of privacy. In this regard, the current permissive use of the Social-Security number as a "universal identifier" should be reconsidered and limits set to protect individual privacy.

Each of these safeguards, where relevant, is to be applied to the *protection of associational privacy* as well as the privacy of persons.

Moreover, the National Data Control Board should encourage, and where necessary financially assist, both the computer industry and its clients to increase computer capacity for protection of confidentiality against both accidents and intentional exposure; and raise professional standards by an intensive program of education for computer handlers in regard to privacy rights and professional handling standards.

Such a law—indeed, even a full-fledged congressional debate of such a law—would encourage a higher degree of self-consciousness about personal and group reserve among both the population in general and the commercial and service industries which routinely handle and process our lives, sometimes rather cavalierly.

Police and government activity

It speaks well for our society that the average citizen does not immediately connect civil-liberties issues with police or government activity. Our history has been relatively free of police-state tactics and preoccupations. But historical good fortune can also cause us to overlook serious denials of civil liberties, which is especially easy if we are white, middle class and politically conventional, until police or government encroachment has taken firm hold in major and perhaps unintended portions of our lives.

Part of the problem is simply that the work of police and government necessarily requires that they invade the privacy of others to seek personal information about them for legal or social-service reasons. How that invasion is conducted, under what restraints, and with what recourse of appeal against the invader become questions that must be answered—and persistently asked in order to require public answers—to determine whether the price paid is worth the service which is rendered by such surveillance.

At first glance, it seems a likely measure to propose the same kind of general oversight board for police and government activity as in the nongovernmental area. But reflection warns us against moving in this direction. The kind of records kept by police and government agencies, such as the FBI, the IRS, and the Defense Intelligence Agency, are so sensitive and so susceptible to political misuse that the issue of privacy maintenance is better handled agency by agency. The inherent dangers of a networking of intelligence systems became evident with the revelation of the famous Huston Plan under consideration by the Nixon administration at the height of its paranoia over domestic "subversives." Specific suggestions, however, for more effective administrative accountability to Congress, and the development of stipulated restrictions on privacy invasion in both law-enforcement and government-service agencies are appropriate and need our attention here.

Take, for example, the area of *domestic intelligence*. I have already made recommendations on the uses of investigative grand juries and informers. To these we should add the following:

1. The gathering of intelligence about domestic political conditions is a task for *civil forces only,* since the only role for military forces in civil disorders is under civilian authority. Therefore, military surveillance must stop, as must the domestic use of the CIA.

2. The Committee on Public Justice suggestion that a special supervisory committee of distinguished citizens and public servants be established to devise guidelines and monitor on an ongoing basis the practice of the several federal agencies now involved in domestic surveillance should be enacted into law. Where jurisdiction permits, all proposed surveillance of political conditions should be cleared through this group, with full administrative and legal penalties for any departure from this standard.

3. Supplementing such a committee, Congress should supervise programs and priorities of agencies involved in domestic surveillance by more firmly exercising its budgetary control, including the use of line-budget reviews.

4. Procedures should be established for access to domestic intelligence files, except under unusual circumstances, by the

person in question (or the group in question), and opportunity given for challenge as to accuracy, correction where indicated, and expungement of unnecessary or obsolete information.

5. To enforce such guidelines, damage-suit procedures and/or dismissal of persons intentionally violating the guidelines should be established. These enforcement proceedings should apply equally to those in high public office, and if abuses are flagrant, they should be considered grounds for possible censure or impeachment.

Concerning *police activity*, the following legislative and administrative initiatives are recommended:

1. Arrest records (without conviction) should be maintained only for a limited period of time and should be strictly confined to law-enforcement use. Any official using such data for other purposes—such as employment, eligibility for housing, welfare, or job training—should be fined or dismissed and the dossiered subject notified for possible recovery of damages. These same restrictions as to access should apply to conviction records.

2. The activity of local police department civil-disobedience and intelligence squads needs much stricter control. Wherever these are presently in operation, or where they become operational in the future, a committee of local distinguished citizens— including representatives of minority groups and civil liberties experts—should be appointed to establish and monitor standards of individual and group privacy. Such a committee should have power to levy fines and bring dismissal charges in cases of intentional violation.

3. The area of the privacy rights of *imprisoned* persons needs thorough revision. A national committee of civil-liberties specialists and affected government employees should be established to devise and monitor a prisoner "bill of rights." This seems particularly urgent at the present moment with mounting evidence that psychosurgical and pharmacological means of behavior modification are of spreading use in prisons and mental hospitals. These new technologies need careful ethical scrutiny and scrupulous protection of prisoner (and patient) rights to privacy, including the personal integrity of mind and body.

4. The computer networking of investigative dossiers between local and national law-enforcement agencies—as proposed in the FBI's National Crime Information Center—with the consequent

de-refinement of file information and threatened loss of confidentiality needs to be more strictly supervised and brought into better balance with rights of personal and group privacy. The suggestion by a recent National Science Foundation task force that such files be put under the care of an "informational trust agency" independent of officials with line-agency responsibility for using the data seems an appropriate safeguard.[12]

Turning to the issue of *governmental service agencies,* many of the specific proposals for the protection of personally sensitive data made in connection with the nongovernmental area also apply here:

1. Social Security, welfare, housing, education (e.g., scholarships, loans, research grants), and medical records should in general enjoy the same rights of subject access, challenge for accuracy or relevancy, and expungement as recommended earlier for the private sector. The type of information sought, the means of seeking it, and the mode of its storage and availability should follow the guidelines set down for nongovernmental use.

2. Service agencies should establish routine procedures for insuring that these privacy rights are protected in the process of data handling. Employees should receive specific training concerning these rules and their breach should be grounds for fine or dismissal.

3. In the preparation of, or the funding of, research programs where personal data is to be collected, government service agencies should take precautions against invasion of personal reserve that is unwarranted in terms of an overriding personal or social benefit, and will in any case insist upon informed consent. In applications for research funding where personal data is to be collected, specific procedures for privacy protection should be part of the application procedure.

4. An agency ombudsman's office should be established to receive inquiries from citizens or groups wishing access to their files. This office should receive complaints and act as an intra-agency advocate for the party claiming abuse of privacy rights.

Having made these proposals for a legislative approach to the protection of privacy, we might assume our task to be finished. But that would leave an enormous, if routine, daily invasion of our personal reserve without consideration.

Containing consumerism

"Let the buyer beware" is an old adage to which we can add a new meaning. Beware not only whether the product is worth its price but also whether the mode of its selling is worth its price. Little has been done thus far to contain to the dimensions of human dignity the strategies of commodity huckstering, despite the fact that much more goes on in the modern marketplace than trading of self-interests. Indeed, the subversion of the self—undermining the self's ability to stand its distance and take cool measure of what is in fact to its benefit—is now an established part of advertising practice. How can we protect ourselves from a consumerism out of control, that time and again shames and trivializes man's self-space by converting it into the raw material of buying and selling?

From the start two profound difficulties must be admitted. *First,* the majority of Americans do not evidently feel themselves misused in this regard. At least they do not complain. Traditional consumer-advocate groups, and more recently women's-liberation organizations, are some of the few exceptions to this. Thus when a cigarette-sized cigar advertises its wares by playing upon the teenage-male identity crisis ("you know who you are") and sexual fears and fantasies, there is no cry of outrage from parents or churches or educators. It all seems a matter of routine, with little transcendent sense of the fundamental misuse of persons as persons involved. The *second* reality is that the means of containing commercialism to humanly compatible dimensions have received little expert reflection, and at first glance present numerous difficulties. Still a preliminary attempt seems in order.

Since the most obvious violations of human dignity for the gaining of commercial advantage appear often on television, where their effectiveness seems increased by the immediacy of contact, some critics have argued for an end to TV advertising. They know this move would also mean the end of independently owned networks and stations. Such critics look instead to a public-broadcasting-type model of television and radio. But recent events, which have thrown the awesome executive political powers of our nation against the TV networks, show the social value of television's independence, a social distance which perhaps only private ownership can insure.

We must also recognize that such ownership seems at the same moment to close the distance between privately financed television and the advertising interests which support it. Independence is gained from government but not from consumerism. Therefore there clearly needs to be an effective "third party" introduced to protect audiences from advertising practices which undermine dignity and trivialize man. The Federal Communications Commission, through its licensing function and periodic renewals, might well be used to monitor and enforce standards of privacy in this regard. Government action recently brought against *Geritol* for "misleading advertising" provides a certain precedent, although the action there was based upon the contents of the product, not the mode of its selling.

Government leverage could strengthen internal corporate committees on "commercial ethics" and give them some weight to resist a single-minded pursuit of growth and profit. These committees might become in-house educational instruments for training in the public responsibility of corporate power—an internal corporate device which socially responsible businessmen have long been looking for.

This process, however, must carefully avoid any kind of new puritan vendetta which would deny that people have legitimate interests in their bodies or in sex. In fact, containing commercial debasement should lead to a new sense of the value and dignity of bodies and sexuality. Carefully drawn guidelines as to areas of protected human reserve would seem an appropriate safeguard.

Finally, the particular means of government supervision must be constructed in such a fashion as to screen out partisan political pressures. The dangers of using the federal-licensing function to police TV (and other media) standards is made clear by the fact that it was only the unlicensed, newsprint media that felt free to do the deep investigative work which eventually surfaced the political scandals of Watergate. Again, careful guidelines should prevent one-sided shifts in policy.

All of this represents only a beginning of what needs to become a society-wide discussion of how to define and control our "quality of life" rather than mindlessly running on in the endless pursuit of a maximum quantity of goods. Clearly part of this quality needs to be freedom for a diversity of life-styles. Unfortunately, the old notion that the sovereign consumer operating in a free-market system would supply this spontaneously has been belied by the undermining of buyer autonomy. The old "automatic hand" needs now a more self-conscious guidance.

And this brings us directly to the other half of our task in this chapter—protecting privacy, yes; but also insuring that *the public is in fact publicly available,* that public "things" are publicly governed.

Keeping the Public World Public

> The First Amendment does not protect a "freedom to speak." It protects the freedom of those activities of thought and communication by which we "govern." It is concerned, not with a private right, but with a public power, a governmental responsibility.[13]
>
> —Professor Alexander Meiklejohn

Privacy has too often been viewed simply as a matter of what an individual has a right to withhold from public scrutiny. Privacy is surely that. But, as Professor Meiklejohn has seen, it is more. Privacy relates to the distribution of power in society, to the forms of public communication by which we govern. Thus, it is not a contradiction, but an extension of the right of personal and group reserve, when we speak also of the *public's right to know.* The more public power a person or institution exercises, the more that person or institution is a legitimate object of public scrutiny.

Secreting power and influence in a society undermines the means by which the people govern. It replaces politics with behind-the-scenes administrative deals. That's why Watergate is such an accurate summary of our present tendency as a society. It illustrates the ambition of the executive power both (1) to unveil the plans and expose the personages of its opposition, and (2) to secret and secure its own hold upon the distribution of public advantages. *Keeping public benefits publicly available* is the second and necessary part of the task argued for in this book. Without this political effect, "privacy protection" becomes merely the cry of the lonely crowd that it be left alone, behind drawn curtains, to enjoy its conventionalities.

How can we go about this task? The insights are not new; only, perhaps, the possibility of in fact acting upon them.

The public's right to know

A very vital part of the political process has been brought under new scrutiny as a result of the Watergate-related revelations regarding campaign expenditures and conflict of interest on the part of public officials. In the next section we will take up the matter of financing the electoral process itself. Here, we might find helpful the provisions of a proposed state election law in Michigan. In addition to calling for full disclosure of political contributions and campaign expenditures, the proposed legislation would require all candidates to identify the sources of all substantial income and to list all assets in excess of $1,000. Also, all lobbyists would be required to identify their clients and to report their expenditures. This legislation could well become a model for other municipal, state, and federal codes. The result would be a making public of the sources of influence upon elected public officials. To such a public disclosure law I would add provisions for public availability of all congressional and administrative agency decisions that have widespread public effect, including open committee meetings, record votes, open access to interagency and intraagency recommendations on issues with important economic or power implications. This publicity would make more difficult secret bargaining and politically lucrative deals on such things as bank and corporate merger applications, TV, radio, and airline licensing, milk and any other price-support decisions, pending antitrust, or IRS and other law-enforcement proceedings All of this should be backed up with stiff penalties—fines, removal from office, and imprisonment—for offenders. Such disclosure laws would help insure that the *public's business takes place publicly.*

Newsmen have a special role in this process, and therefore require *special protection.* Because of recent Supreme Court decisions the news reporter finds himself at present without legal protection as to his sources. The result, as Senator Weicker of Connecticut has said, is that "our system of checks and balances is becoming more unchecked and more unbalanced." Because it is the free flow of news that is, as the senator says, "the best guarantee that nobody steals America." In an age of massive government money and power, and the daily demonstration of behind-the-scenes political pandering to special interests, the system of the public's "right to know" is a crucial indicator of freedom's preservation—or its loss.

Congress should enact legislation in this regard to provide news professionals with an "absolute" protection from being compelled to reveal their sources, except where there is reason to believe that foreign espionage or aggression is involved. Such a policy would protect society in its extremities while closing the door on prosecutorial and government "fishing expeditions" which now expose newsmen to the dilemmas of legal jeopardy and so threaten to dry up the protected news sources necessary to a politically vital and probing press. Thomas Jefferson's comment about the value of the news media is very appropriate, "Were it left to me to decide whether we should have a Government without newspapers or newspapers without Government, I should not hesitate to prefer the latter." The adequate protection of the system of free news reporting is vital to our democratic process. An attack upon that system by government officials smacks of despotism and should be squarely blocked by both law and public outrage.

But this "right to know" cannot stand alone in preserving public transactions as publicly available. It needs the supplement of a *public way of financing the public's elections.*

Publicly financed elections

The National Advisory Commission of Criminal Justice, established by the Nixon administration, came to the conclusion not long ago that government corruption, as they said, "stands as a serious impediment to the task of reducing criminality in America." The commission's research showed that so long as official corruption flourishes, "the war against crime will be perceived by many as a war of the powerful against the powerless, 'law and order' will be a hypocritical rallying cry, and 'equal justice under law' will be an empty phrase."[14]

Cynicism breeds contempt for society, contempt for the normal civility we depend upon to function as social creatures. In order that its instruction no longer *begin from the top,* the commission suggested a stringent set of public disclosure laws similar to those I have listed above. But it went further. "The commission recognizes," the report continued, "the electoral process as a major source of corruption." Detailing its findings, the commission concluded that, "dependence on a source of campaign funding represents the most pervasive and constant pecuniary shackle on the judgment and action of elected officials."[15]

George A. Sprater, chairman of American Airlines, a firm which has admitted making an illegal corporate contribution to President Nixon's 1972 campaign, put the case from the donor's side. He said, "A large part of the money raised from the business community for political purposes is given in fear of what would happen if it were not given." [16] Whether out of fear of postelection regulatory agency retaliation or, as surely is often the case, out of the promise of especially friendly handling, this central source of privatizing public power into behind-the-scene "big deals" needs now to be firmly blocked. What we need is *full public financing of election campaigns*, from the municipal through the federal levels.

Those who argue for a middle position—for example, strictly enforced limits on campaign expenditures and also on size of contributions—fail to take into account the inordinate difficulty this puts upon a nonincumbent. Often relatively unknown, he or she would be faced with the insuperable task of raising hundreds of thousands (minimum budget for a U.S. House race) or even millions (for a Senate race) of dollars in small donations. The sheer size of such a fund-raising undertaking would itself represent an expense few could meet. We must conclude therefore that the only workable answer seems to be a broad system of complete public financing. Senators Kennedy and Scott, and Senators Stevenson and Mathias have proposed two versions of such a law, and the prospects for passage—if public attention remains well focused— seem promising.

Such a bill should include the following:

1. To insure that a candidate be serious and have at least a credible public following, a minimum of private fund raising should be required. Senator Cranston of California has suggested that $2,500 for a House race, $10,000 for a senatorial race, and $100,000 for a presidential candidate be privately collected before public financing becomes operative. This requirement would prevent a senseless proliferation of candidates while not closing the door to third or fourth party aspirants. To strengthen this "viable candidacy" requirement, the maximum size of individual donations allowed should be $100.

2. Strict limits on permissible campaign spending should be imposed; for example, ten cents per person of voting age per state in a presidential primary, and fifteen cents on the same basis in a general election. In proportions equivalent to size of effort, similar restrictions should be imposed upon all federal, state, and municipal elections. Systematic violations of this provision

should be cause for removal from office if the candidate is elected, and normal legal penalties of fine and/or imprisonment should be levied.

Given these stipulations, the federal government should thereupon supply all funds, beyond the initial qualifying sum, to run for public office. This public financing of the public's system of election would go a long way toward squeezing off the secreting of public power into behind-the-scene payoffs by organized interest groups or politically generous "fat cats."

But clearly it is not enough just to take private money out of the public's business of electing its public servants. So long as the wholly inordinate distribution of wealth continues in our country (see chapter 2), the actual lines of political power and influence will remain narrowly drawn. As Professor Edwin Kuh of MIT has said, "Massive concentrations of wealth or income make a mockery of political democracy. . . . 'One person, one vote' is a sham—for the middle class and poor alike—when the rich can buy political influence." [17] Under the present circumstance of wealth and power in our nation "power to the people" becomes ironically a radical statement. "Freedom," "government by consent of the governed"—these rallying cries become once again, as at the birth of our country, heavily laden with implications for fundamental structural changes in our society. However, the politics of income redistribution clearly must begin with public-financed elections of those whose responsibility it is to write and rewrite our tax and estate laws. Election reform would be at least a beginning of the wider social task of pursuing greater equality in what has become in fact a steeply unequal society.

Other suggestions for opening up the process of public decision making include reform of the committee and seniority systems in Congress, reform of the party caucus, and revision of legislative and executive "conflict of interest" guidelines to reflect more accurately the danger of preferential treatment by self-interested legislators. Most of these suggestions have been around a long time and are widely known. But this may be a particularly happy moment for the translating of pious intentions into law.

Bureaucratic independence

One means, however, of bringing public discipline to bear upon the public's business has received little formal notice. That is the strengthening of bureaucratic independence to interpose, between the interests of the general public and any private tampering by powerful government officials, a "professional" line of resistance. The value of such bureaucratic interposition was demonstrated by a quite astonishing phenomenon in the early 1970s. Government bureaucracy began to spring massive "leaks." Information that powerful administrators wanted secreted became available to the public. The "little gray men" of conspicuous anonymity suddenly became a major "plumbing" problem for the ambitions of executive management. But bureaucracy does not usually show its potential for protecting freedom by such striking means. More often it is done by quiet bureaucratic stubbornness—and the civil-service protection that makes it possible—before attempted personal misuse of public power. Precisely this idea first gave birth to the idea of a "neutral civil service."

The development of a professional government bureaucracy, screened from the passing political parade, originated a century ago when the Jacksonian principle of "rotation of office" had degenerated into a widespread "spoils system."[18] Civil-service reformers used the idea of a "science of public administration" to establish a sharp dichotomy—or what was presumed to be—between politics and administration. More recently, empirical studies have shown how administrative agencies have in fact fallen under the tutelage of those they administer, for example, the Department of Agriculture serving the interests of agri-business, the Food and Drug Administration dominated by large pharmaceutical companies, the U.S. Department of Commerce subservient to the needs of multi-national conglomerates, and so on.

Still, this debunking of the notion of a neutral "science" of social administration only makes more obvious the need to *define grounds* for maintaining distance between politics and professional government bureaucracy. My suggestion is that in a democratic society, or one that aspires to be, government bureaucracy's allegiance is fundamentally "to the people." Bureaucracy can be an instrument protected against the immediate political storms to insure that governing authority actually remains in the hands of the governed rather than being fictionalized by a clandestine buddy system. Civil service *stands in for the people*—or should—*between elections.* Its responsibility to defend itself rests upon this independent duty to the body politic.

Thus, bureaucrats have a normative function. They have been appointed to help in the *task of self-government.*

Thus, in extreme situations, the unauthorized exposure to public attention of the twisting of administrative agency power to private advantage remains, nevertheless, thoroughly in the tradition of civil service "decorum." These unusual practices, however, need obviously to be replaced wherever possible with routine procedures for insuring bureaucratic independence—procedures of record keeping, for example, such as those introduced in the Department of Justice by then Attorney General Elliot Richardson. Under those rules, all contacts from legislative or executive offices had to be formally noted in memo and summarized as to content. This same procedure as applied to other administrative agencies would bring some discipline upon inordinate outside influence. Similarly, codes of professional ethics with built-in incentives, established standards of independence as to judgment of the "common" or "public good," would improve the reputation of bureaucracy in protecting the rule of the people. A very important contribution to public trust, for example, was made by the Pentagon cost analyst, who stood his ground against aircraft company cost overruns, lost his job because of it, and then was reinstated by the Civil Service Commission. I would recommend that in such cases the commission have independent authority to mandate promotion and salary increment and to bring charges of culpable mismanagement of public funds against offending hierarchs, including the military.

Clearly, much needs to be done in terms of appointment, promotion, and accountability to achieve greater autonomy between administrative agencies and those they administer. But just as clearly, here is a potentially powerful weapon—sometimes already at work and with little public gratitude—for the everyday guarding of the public realm as a place where the public's business is transacted without subversion by an oligarchy hidden behind the facade of democratic elections. Keeping the public world in public is a matter of political reform of the electoral process, but it is also a matter of bureaucratic reform of the nonelectoral domain of government.

A Matter of Spirit

But all such legislative and administrative reforms remain dependent finally upon *a quality of the common life,* a quality of care. This texture of common concern shapes the actual context of possibilities both of the practice of corruption and of the reform of corruption. This common, or public, concern is, so to speak, the *final limit setter.* Upon its decision most of the rest depends. Curiously, we hardly have a language in political science or ethics to talk about it. Man remains as he began, a "meaning" creature, constituted more of spirit than of self-interest. The reverence we bear our own and each other's souls in the long run weighs most. What we want to "mean" is what counts.

Freedom and dignity—the goal and purpose of seeking a private man in a public world—remain fragile accomplishments. They depend upon rules and conventions and self-restraints most of which cannot be systematically supervised. They depend upon persons who have many opportunities of corruption and are daily exposed to the retribution of angered interests and powers. In the, end they depend upon the few who stay alert and who are able when necessary to pay prices, and upon the many who pay their prices in other ways but are willing to say "no" when the trespass of liberty becomes sufficiently blatant and the times sufficiently critical.

Notes

Chapter 1

[1] Franz Kafka, *The Trial* (New York: Alfred A. Knopf, Inc., 1964), pp. 198-199.

[2] Charles Horton Cooley, *Social Organization* (New York: Schocken Books Inc., 1962), p. 343.

[3] Allan F. Westin, in *Privacy and Freedom* (New York: Atheneum Publishers, 1967), presents an excellent summary of this anthropological evidence in his first chapter.

[4] These three cases are all documented in the FBI Media Files as published in *Win*, vol. 8, nos. 4 and 5 (March 1 and 15, 1972). The college is Swarthmore, and the U.S. Congressman is Henry S. Reuss of Wisconsin.

[5] *Congressional Record*, February 3, 1970, vol. 116, part 2, p. 2227.

[6] *Win, op. cit.*, p. 28.

[7] Sidney M. Jourard, "Some Psychological Aspects of Privacy," *Law and Contemporary Problems* (publication of Duke University School of Law), vol. 31, no. 2 (Spring, 1966), p. 313.

[8] Quoted by Thomas I. Emerson in *The System of Freedom of Expression* (New York: Random House, Inc., 1970), p. 546.

[9] *Ibid.*, p. 545.

[10] Jourard, *op. cit.*, p. 312.

[11] Edward Shils, "Privacy: Its Constitution and Vicissitudes," *Law and Contemporary Problems*, vol. 31, no. 2 (Spring, 1966), p. 306.

[12] *Congressional Record*, September 8, 1970, vol. 116, part 23, p. 30793.

[13] Alexis de Tocqueville, *Democracy in America* (New York: Vintage Books, Random House, Inc., 1945), vol. 2, p. 118.

[14] Westin, *op. cit.*, pp. 350-351.

[15] *Ibid.*, p. 398.

[16] Quoted from a *New York Times* summary, June 20, 1972, p. 23.

[17] Karl Mannheim, *Ideology and Utopia* (New York: Harcourt Brace Jovanovich, Inc., 1936), pp. 118-119.

[18] *Davies Warehouse Company* v. *Bowles,* in Arthur R. Miller, *The Assault on Privacy* (Ann Arbor: The University of Michigan Press, 1971), p. 146.

[19] Michael Harrington, *Toward a Democratic Left* (New York: The Macmillan Company, 1968), p. 144.

[20] Ralph Nader, "The Dossier Invades the Home," *Saturday Review,* vol. 54, no. 16 (April 17, 1971), pp. 18 ff.

[21] Miller, *op. cit.,* pp. 95-96.

[22] Staff Report No. 92—554, Subcommittee on Constitutional Rights of the Committee on the Judiciary, U.S. Senate, December 6, 1971, p. 22.

[23] Miller, *op. cit.,* p. 34.

[24] "The Theory and Practice of American Political Intelligence," *The New York Review of Books,* vol. 14, no. 7 (April 22, 1971), p. 27.

[25] *Win, op. cit.,* p. 70.

[26] *Hearings Before the Subcommittee on Constitutional Rights of the Committee on the Judiciary, U.S. Senate* (Feb.-Mar., 1971), Part 1, p. 765.

[27] *New York Times,* December 17, 1970, p. 1.

[28] "State of Siege," *New York Times Magazine,* July 22, 1973, p. 10.

[29] Miller, *op. cit.,* p. 204.

Chapter 2

[1] From S. K. Padover, *A Jefferson Profile as Revealed in His Letters* (New York: The John Day Company, Inc., 1956), pp. 272-273.

[2] Alexis de Tocqueville, *Democracy in America* (New York: Vintage Books, Random House, Inc., 1945), vol. 2, p. 116.

[3] Reinhold Niebuhr, *Moral Man and Immoral Society* (New York: Charles Scribner's Sons, 1932), p. 8.

[4] John Kenneth Galbraith, *The New Industrial State* (Boston: Houghton Mifflin Company, 1967), *passim.* Galbraith, however, makes the mistake of viewing much too sanguinely the economic situation of the middle class and so is left without a politics. He looks instead to the aesthetic sophistication of the technical elite.

[5] Hannah Arendt, "Lying in Politics: Reflections on the Pentagon Papers," *Crises of the Republic* (New York: Harcourt Brace Jovanovich, Inc., 1972).

[6] John Scharr, "Legitimacy in the Modern State," *Power and Community: Dissenting Essays in Political Science,* ed. Philip Green and Sanford Levinson (New York: Pantheon Books, Inc., 1970), pp. 285-286.

[7] Jacob M. Edelman, *The Symbolic Uses of Politics* (Urbana: University of Illinois Press, 1967), *passim.*

[8] Lee Soltow, ed., *Six Papers on the Size Distribution of Wealth and Income* (New York: Bureau of Economic Research, Inc., 1969), p. 122.

[9] Karl Mannheim, *Ideology and Utopia* (New York: Harcourt Brace Jovanovich, Inc., 1936) pp. 21-22.

[10] "And Now a Word from Mr. & Mrs. Middle," *New York Times,* "The Week in Review," July 23, 1972.

[11] *New York Times,* November 18, 1968, p. 38.

[12] Richard Sennett and Jonathan Cobb, *The Hidden Injuries of Class* (New York: Alfred A. Knopf, Inc., 1972), *passim.*

[13] B. F. Skinner, *Beyond Freedom and Dignity* (New York: Alfred A. Knopf, Inc., 1971), pp. 3-5.

[14] *Ibid.*, p. 181.

[15] *Ibid.*, p. 18.

[16] *Ibid.*, p. 81.

[17] *Ibid.*, pp. 205-206.

[18] *Ibid.*, p. 208.

[19] *Ibid.*, p. 43.

[20] Gibson Winter, in his *Elements for a Social Ethic* (New York: The Macmillan Company, 1971), provides a detailed analysis of this mistake of moving uncritically between levels of social analysis and policy prescription. See especially chapters 2-6.

[21] Skinner, *op. cit.*, p. 210.

[22] Amitai Etzioni, *The Active Society* (New York: The Free Press, 1968), p. 5, italics added.

Chapter 3

[1] Ernest Becker, *The Structure of Evil* (New York: George Braziller, Inc., 1968), p. 184. Reprinted with the permission of the publishers. Copyright © by Ernest Becker.

[2] I use the phrase "inner space" in a nontheoretical way. It should not be confused with the special use the psychiatrist Erik Erickson makes of it in his peculiar views of "femininity."

[3] Ernest Becker, *The Birth and Death of Meaning* (New York: The Free Press, 1971), p. 4.

[4] *Ibid.*, p. 16.

[5] *Ibid.*

[6] *The Social Psychology of George Herbert Mead*, ed. Anselm Strauss (Chicago: University of Chicago Press, 1956), p. 217.

[7] Erving Goffman, *The Presentation of Self in Everyday Life* (Garden City, N.Y.: Anchor Books, Doubleday & Company, Inc., 1959), *passim.*

[8] See Erving Goffman, *Asylums* (Garden City, N.Y.: Anchor Books, Doubleday & Company, Inc., 1961), *passim.*

[9] Becker, *The Birth and Death of Meaning*, p. 106.

[10] Sartre develops this analysis of the relationship of consciousness and body in *Being and Nothingness.*

[11] This advertisement appeared in the *New York Times*, January 20, 1970.

[12] Thomas S. Szasz, *The Myth of Mental Illness* (New York: Harper & Row, Publishers, 1961).

[13] Goffman, *Asylums*, p. 28.

[14] *Ibid.*, p. 169.

[15] Arthur R. Miller, *The Assault on Privacy* (Ann Arbor: The University of Michigan Press, 1971), p. 49.

[16] From Alan F. Westin and Michael A. Baker, *Databanks in a Free Society* (New York: Quadrangle Books, Inc., 1972).

[17] Kenneth Keniston, *The Uncommitted: Alienated youth in American society* (New York: Harcourt Brace Jovanovich, Inc., 1965), p. 446.

[18] John Calvin, *Institutes of the Christian Religion* (Grand Rapids: Wm. B. Eerdmans Publishing Company, 1966), vol. 2, chap. 7, p. 7.

[19] Loren C. Eiseley, *The Unexpected Universe* (New York: Harcourt Brace Jovanovich, Inc., 1969), is especially good on this.

[20] Paul Tillich, *The Courage to Be* (New Haven: Yale University Press, 1952), p. 73.

[21] Max Stirner, *The Ego and His Own*, trans. Steven T. Byington (New York: Libertarian Book Club, 1963), p. 320.

[22] J. Glenn Gray, *The Warriors* (New York: Harcourt Brace Jovanovich, Inc., 1959), pp. 241-242.

[23] *The Works of Ralph Waldo Emerson* (New York: Tudor Publishing Company, 1937), p. 46.

[24] *Ibid.*, p. 31.

[25] *Ibid.*, p. 55.

[26] *Ibid.*, p.48.

[27] See page 54 of chapter 2.

Chapter 4

[1] Jean-Jacques Rousseau, *The Social Contract*, ed. and trans. Charles Frankel (New York: Hafner Publishing Co., Inc., 1947), bk. 1, chap. 8, p. 18.

[2] Edmund Burke, *Reflections on the Revolution in France* (New York: P. F. Collier, Inc., 1909), pp. 244-245.

[3] Michael Walzer, *Obligations: Essays on Disobedience, War, and Citizenship* (Cambridge: Harvard University Press, 1970), p. 201.

[4] C. Wright Mills, *The Power Elite* (New York: Oxford University Press, Inc., 1957), p. 306.

[5] "Privacy in the First Amendment," *Yale Law Journal*, vol. 82, no. 7 (June, 1973), p. 1465, italics added.

[6] *U.S.* v. *Caldwell*, 408 U.S. 665 (1972) quoted in *ibid.*, p. 1464.

[7] Quoted by Paul Cowan in "The New Grand Jury," *New York Times Magazine*, April 29, 1973, p. 38.

[8] Walzer, *op. cit.*, p. 140.

[9] Cowan, *op. cit.*, p. 36.

[10] Albert Camus, *Resistance, Rebellion, and Death*, trans. Justin O'Brien (New York: Modern Library, Inc., 1960), p. 77.

[11] Cowan, *op. cit.*, p. 38.

[12] *Win*, vol. 8, nos. 4 and 5 (March 1 and 15, 1972), p. 52.

[13] See *Philadelphia Evening Bulletin*, February and March, 1973.

[14] The sources for this illustration are taken from various Philadelphia newspapers beginning in August, 1973.

[15] John Scharr, "Legitimacy in the Modern State," *Power and Community: Dissenting Essays in Political Science*, ed. Philip Green and Sanford Levinson (New York: Pantheon Books, Inc., 1970), p. 300.

[16] Two books by John Kenneth Galbraith analyze this process clearly, his previously mentioned *The New Industrial State* and his more recent volume, *Economics and the Public Purpose*. In both he argues that *all* advanced industrial

societies respond to the same central directive—the needs of the administrative "technostructure" for predictable growth and the marginalizing of risk.

[17] "Bureaucracy," *From Max Weber*, ed. H. H. Gerth and C. Wright Mills (New York: Oxford University Press, Inc., 1946), pp. 212-213.

[18] Ivan Illich, *Tools for Conviviality* (New York: Harper & Row, Publishers, 1973), pp. 10-11.

[19] *Ibid.*, p. 52.

[20] *Ibid.*, pp. 54 and 57.

[21] *Ibid.*, p. 11.

[22] Richard Sennett, *The Uses of Disorder: Personal Identity & City Life* (New York: Alfred A. Knopf, Inc., 1970), p. 196.

Chapter 5

[1] Quoted in Ernest Becker, *The Structure of Evil* (New York: George Braziller, Inc., 1968), p. 3.

[2] See Pierre Teilhard de Chardin's *The Phenomenon of Man* (New York: Harper & Row, Publishers, 1959) for the full presentation of this argument.

[3] Hannah Arendt, *The Human Condition* (Garden City, N.Y.: Anchor Books, Doubleday & Company, Inc., 1958), p. 209.

[4] I have borrowed some of this analysis from Max Weber's typology of religious theodicies in *The Sociology of Religion.*

[5] Karl Marx, *Economic and Philosophical Manuscripts*, trans. T. B. Bottomore, in *Marx's Concept of Man*, ed. Erich Fromm (New York: Frederick Ungar Publishing Co., Inc., 1966), p. 96.

[6] Max Weber, *The Methodology of the Social Sciences* (New York: The Free Press, 1949), p. 112.

[7] H. Richard Niebuhr, *The Responsible Self* (New York: Harper & Row, Publishers, 1963), p. 112.

[8] Becker, *op. cit.*, p. 171, italics added.

[9] William James, *Essays in Pragmatism* (New York: Hafner Publishing Co., Inc., 1949), p. 83.

[10] Charles Hampden-Turner, *Radical Man* (Cambridge: Schenkman Publishing Co., Inc., 1970), p. 47.

[11] John Scharr, "Legitimacy in the Modern State," *Power and Community: Dissenting Essays in Political Science*, ed. Philip Green and Sanford Levinson (New York: Pantheon Books, Inc., 1970), p. 287.

[12] Much of the material on these two issues was prepared by Dean Kelley of the National Council of Churches for a special Task Force on Privacy organized by the United Presbyterian Church in the U.S.A.

[13] *New York Times Magazine*, September 2, 1972, p. 21.

[14] Louise Brown, "The IRS: Taxation with Misrepresentation," *The Progressive*, vol. 37, no. 10 (October, 1973), p. 27.

[15] *Win*, vol. 8, nos. 4 and 5 (March 1 and 15, 1972), p. 49. In justifying such actions, banks often contend that financial records are the property of the bank and not of the depositor. The bank has complete control of them. The same argument is sometimes put forward by educational institutions concerning grade and testing records, occasionally even counseling dossiers.

[16] Quoted from a private memorandum written for the Task Force on Privacy, sponsored by the United Presbyterian Church in the U.S.A.

[17] The definitive treatment of this issue is Fred Kuhlmann's "Communications to Clergymen—When Are They Privileged?" in *Valparaiso University Law Review* (Spring, 1968).

[18] Quoted from *ibid.*, p. 287.

[19] *Ibid.*, p. 289.

Chapter 6

[1] I am particularly dependent in this section upon the instruction I received from my legal colleagues on the Task Force on Privacy, organized by the Presbyterian Church in the U.S.A. Especially helpful were Professor Travis Lewin of Syracuse University Law School and Hope Eastman, Esquire, of the Washington National Office of ACLU.

[2] Quoted from Alan F. Westin, *Privacy and Freedom* (New York: Atheneum Publishers, 1967), p. 336.

[3] *Ibid.*, p. 332.

[4] *Ibid.*, p. 346.

[5] See Alan F. Westin and Michael A. Baker, *Databanks in a Free Society* (New York: Quadrangle Books, Inc., 1972), p. 18.

[6] Westin, *Privacy and Freedom*, p. 353.

[7] *Ibid.*

[8] *Ibid.*, p. 51.

[9] *Ibid.*, pp. 350-351.

[10] Cited in memorandum to author from Professor Travis Lewin of Syracuse University.

[11] *Business Week*, no. 2300 (October 6, 1973), p. 93.

[12] See Westin and Baker, *Databanks*, p. 400.

[13] Quoted in "Privacy in the First Amendment," Yale Law Journal, vol. 82, no. 7 (June, 1973), p. 1464.

[14] "Nixon Panel Says Official Corruption Impedes Nation's Effort to Curb Crime," *New York Times*, August 19, 1973, p. 41.

[15] *Ibid.*

[16] Quoted from lead editorial in the *Detroit Free Press*, October 19, 1973.

[17] "The Robin Hood Syndrome," *New York Times*, March 5, 1973, p. 29.

[18] John Rohr, "Ethics for Bureaucrats," *America*, vol. 128, no. 20 (May 26, 1973), p. 489. In this article, Rohr addresses some of these issues.

INDEX